FOOTSTEPS  EVERY DAY

LUKE
A Devotional Commentary

BOB ROGNLIEN

Footsteps Every Day, Volume Three
Luke: A Devotional Commentary
Copyright © Bob Rognlien 2023

All rights reserved. No part of this book may be reproduced without written permission, except for brief quotations in books and reviews. For information contact GX Books, bobrognlien@gmail.com or www.bobrognlien.com.

All Scripture quotations are from the Christian Standard Bible® (CSB®), Copyright © 2017 by Holman Bible Publishers. Used by permission. Christian Standard Bible® and CSB® are federally registered trademarks of Holman Bible Publishers.

Cover Design: Timothy J. Bergren
Book Design: Amit Dey
Editor: Robert Neely
ISBN: 978-0-9815247-9-5
Published by GX Books

DEDICATION

To my sister Leslie,
who has always been
my best friend and closest ally.
Your unshakeable loyalty,
your unconditional love,
and your uncompromising character
inspire me every day to become more like Jesus.

ACKNOWLEDGEMENTS

I want to express my gratitude to all those who supported me, prayed for me, and made the writing of this book and series possible. Specifically, I want to thank Pam Rognlien, Chris Pudel, and Heidi Hollings for carefully rooting out my many mistakes. Any that remain are mine alone. Thanks to Robert Neely for editing the manuscript and Amit Dey for designing the interior pages. They have both made the book eminently more readable. Special thanks to Tim Bergren for designing another great book cover. Above all I give thanks to Jesus, the Great Shepherd of the Sheep, who continues inviting us all to listen to his voice and follow him by taking steps of faith every day. To him be all the glory!

INTRODUCTION

In the first chapter of his Gospel, Mark describes Jesus' predictable pattern of spending time alone with his heavenly Father the King. *Very early in the morning, while it was still dark, he got up, went out, and made his way to a deserted place; and there he was praying.* (Mark 1:35)

Those who follow Jesus recognize this is a critical rhythm of discipleship—seeking to become more like him by hearing and responding to what he is saying every day. Paul says, *"So faith comes from what is heard, and what is heard comes through the message about Christ."* (Romans 10:17) When we listen for the voice of Jesus speaking through his written Word, the Holy Spirit plants faith in our hearts. When we exercise that faith by taking a concrete step in the footsteps of Jesus, we grow as his fruitful disciples and learn to live a more Jesus-shaped life.

Footsteps Every Day is a series of devotional commentaries on the New Testament, designed to help followers of Jesus establish a regular pattern of spending time alone with God, reading Scripture, listening in prayer, and responding with a step of faith. Volume Three, *Luke,* is the third in the series and offers brief reflections on 90 passages that make up Luke's account of Jesus' life, drawing on history, archaeology, and culture to illuminate the Way of Jesus and help you follow him with concrete steps of faith.

Each of these devotional commentaries can be read on its own at your own pace, or you can read all four Gospels in succession. If you read six passages a week, the first four volumes will take you on an incredible year-long journey through the Gospels, following the life of Jesus and reflecting on every recorded thing he said and did during his life on earth!

These books can be used as biblical commentaries by looking up a specific passage you are studying to gain fresh insights from the historical and cultural background to inform you as you teach others and apply God's

Word to daily life. They can also be a great resource for small groups, Bible studies, and classes who are focusing on one or more of the Gospels.

Here are my recommendations for a fruitful devotional journey in Jesus' *Footsteps Every Day*:

- Pick a time in which you have the highest likelihood of being consistent each day. Set aside at least 15 minutes, or better 30 minutes.
- Pick a place where you will be the least distracted and interrupted. Make yourself comfortable but adopt an attentive posture. Get too comfortable and you will fall asleep!
- Read the Scripture passage in your own Bible. My writing is based on the text from the Christian Standard Bible, an excellent and often overlooked translation, but you can use any version you find helpful. Read it again.
- Take some time to prayerfully listen as you scan over the passage, noting what God seems to be pointing out to you.
- Highlight important phrases and make relevant notes in the margins. (Even digital Bibles allow for this. I use the Olive Tree app.)
- Read the commentary provided in *Footsteps Every Day*.
- Prayerfully ask God what he is saying to you through all the above. Listen and write down what is coming to you in the space provided (or type it as a digital note if you are reading the eBook edition).
- Then ask God to show you the next step of faith he wants you to take.
- Write down your step of faith in the space provided (or type it as a digital note if you are reading the eBook edition).
- Take that step of faith!
- If you are having trouble taking that step, share it with someone you trust and ask them to pray for you to exercise the faith God is giving you. Take that step of faith!
- Rinse and repeat!

- At the end of every six days, there is a section called "Footsteps Every Week." Use this space to reflect on the readings from the past week, summarize your insights from each day, identify any major themes, consider any new predictable patterns God is calling you to establish, and identify the most significant verse to memorize.

When we read God's Word and listen to what Jesus is saying to us through the Spirit, it produces faith in our hearts. Our role is to respond to what Jesus is saying by exercising that faith, taking the next step in following the footsteps of Jesus. We are not trying to change ourselves by moral willpower, but rather are putting ourselves in the place where God's Spirit can transform us from the inside out and produce through us good fruit that lasts. This is what it means to live as a Jesus-shaped disciple. Please don't approach this as a religious task that you must perform but receive this opportunity as a gracious invitation to draw near to Jesus, hear his voice, and follow where he leads you on this great adventure of discipleship!

DAY 1

READ AND LISTEN: LUKE 1:1-4

Take a minute to listen for what the Spirit is saying in these verses…

COMMENT AND CONSIDER

Luke was a Gentile physician who met Paul and his disciples in Alexandria Troas on the west coast of modern-day Turkey during the second missional journey. (See Acts 16:10 where Luke's narrative shifts from "they" to "we"). We don't know if Luke was already a believer when they met, but we know that he became one of Paul's closest disciples. Some believe Luke lived in Philippi, because he traveled there from Troas with Paul and then stayed until Paul returned to Philippi a few years later on his way back to Jerusalem at the end of the third missional journey. (See Acts 20:6.)

From that point on, Luke remained with Paul through his arrest in Jerusalem, his imprisonment under the Roman Governors Felix and Festus in Caesarea on the coast of Judea, and all the way to his house imprisonment in Rome at the end of the book of Acts. Luke was still Paul's faithful companion during his final imprisonment in Rome, shortly before his execution, probably by the Emperor Nero. (See 2 Timothy 4:11.) Luke wrote his Gospel as the first volume of a two-volume work, followed by the Acts of the Apostles.

Luke dedicates his two-volume narrative to the *"most honorable Theophilus,"* a title usually reserved for upper class people of means and position. It seems as though Theophilus was a newer believer who supported Luke's efforts to write a more comprehensive and accurate account of what Jesus said and did during his 33 or so years on earth. *"Theophilus"* is a Greek name, indicating he was most likely a Gentile, possibly a wealthy business owner or even a Roman official. Luke is the only Gentile author of a biblical book, so it is not surprising he puts a special emphasis on Jesus' teaching that the Kingdom of God is for Jews and Gentiles alike.

Luke recognizes that others had compiled the eyewitness accounts of Jesus' life, but he indicates his approach was more systematic by stating he *"carefully investigated"* these events in order to write *"an orderly sequence."* Although Luke was not one of Jesus' twelve disciples, he clearly received his information from those who were eyewitnesses, probably interviewing as many as he could during the two years of Paul's imprisonment on the coast of Israel. More than the other Gospel writers, Luke carefully set his narrative in the context of major historical figures, such as King Herod (1:5), Caesar Augustus (2:1), Quirinus the Roman governor of Syria (2:2), Tiberius Caesar, Pontius Pilate, Herod Antipas, Herod Philip, and the High Priests Annas and Caiaphas (3:1-2).

Luke's purpose in writing the Gospel is clear. He wanted Theophilus and others, including us, to become more certain of the words of Jesus and the events of his life so we can follow him more closely and share the Good News of the Kingdom with greater confidence. This marked a major shift from relying on the oral accounts of Jesus' words and actions relayed by the Apostles who witnessed them or others who passed on what they heard from these eyewitnesses. Luke wanted everyone to be able to hear an accurate account of Jesus' life, regardless of whether they were able to receive it directly from an eyewitness. And so he researched the incredible story by asking those eyewitnesses what they heard with their own ears and saw with their own eyes, and he wrote it all down in this orderly account for us.

Imagine if Luke and the other Gospel writers had never written down the apostolic witness. We would be relying on traditions about Jesus passed down innumerable times with highly dubious accuracy. Instead, we have a clearly written account of the eyewitness testimony of the most extraordinary life ever lived and the most powerful teaching ever given, which constitutes the greatest Good News this world has ever known!

How much do you value the Word of God? How easily do you take it for granted? How can a renewed wonder for the gift of the Bible motivate your reading of the Gospel of Luke in the coming weeks?

REFLECT AND RESPOND

What is Jesus saying to me right now?

What step of faith is Jesus calling me to take today?

DAY 2

READ AND LISTEN: LUKE 1:5-25

Take a minute to listen for what the Spirit is saying in these verses…

COMMENT AND CONSIDER

Mark begins his Gospel with Jesus' baptism and temptation. Matthew begins with the conception of Jesus. But Luke takes it back one step further to the conception of John the Baptist. Luke frames the beginning of his story at the end of the reign of Herod the Great, who ruled over the Roman provinces of Idumea, Judea, Samaria, Galilee, Gaulanitus, Trachonitus, and Perea from 37 to 4 BC. Luke introduces us to Elizabeth, a relative of Mary who came from a priestly family, and her husband Zechariah, who served as a priest in the division of Abijah. They lived somewhere west of Jerusalem in the hill country of Judea. Luke tells us they were elderly and childless.

The priests of Israel were divided into 24 divisions, and they lived throughout the land, but they came to Jerusalem twice a year to serve in the Temple for one week at a time. During that week (called a "course") they were busy carrying out the normal functions of the Temple, including the slaughter of animals, the ritual sprinkling of blood, and the burning of offerings on the huge outdoor altar. Each day one of the priests was chosen by lots (like rolling dice) to enter the Sanctuary, the Temple building itself, and replenish the incense which burned continually as a symbol of the prayers rising before God day and night. This was a rare privilege since thousands of priests served in the Temple at any given time. A typical priest might be chosen to go into the Temple only once or twice in his lifetime.

Luke tells us Zechariah was serving one of his week-long courses in the Temple and was chosen by lot to enter the Sanctuary to replenish the incense. When Zechariah entered the Temple, he would have been in awe of the golden decorations covering the inside, the intricately woven curtain at the far end separating the Holy of Holies, the golden lampstand, the golden table for the showbread, and the altar of incense. Outside the other priests led a worship service in the Court of the Women and waited for Zechariah to complete his task.

Then the angel Gabriel appeared to Zechariah beside the altar of incense and delivered the incredibly good news that he and Elizabeth would conceive a son and name him John. Gabriel went on to tell him this special child would be filled with the Spirit even before birth and would prepare the way for the Messiah by turning the hearts of God's people in the spirit and power of Elijah. When Zechariah questioned all this, Gabriel told him he would be struck mute until the baby was born.

There are two named angels in the Bible. Gabriel appears primarily as a messenger from God, while Michael appears primarily as the leader of the heavenly armies of God. It is good to remember that biblical angels are not lovely ladies in flowing dresses or pudgy children with wings, but terrifying heavenly beings who constantly tell people not to be afraid! When Zechariah finally emerged from the Temple unable to speak, the other priests realized he had experienced a supernatural encounter. Luke tells us that exactly what Gabriel prophesied came to pass, and Elizabeth became pregnant in her old age! She recognized this as a miracle from God saying, *"The Lord has done this for me."*

Are there things in your life that you long for but have given up on and stopped praying for? Are there promises God has made that you find difficult to believe? What does Zechariah and Elizabeth's experience demonstrate? What can we learn from their different responses?

REFLECT AND RESPOND
What is Jesus saying to me right now?

What step of faith is Jesus calling me to take today?

DAY 3

READ AND LISTEN: LUKE 1:26-38
Take a minute to listen for what the Spirit is saying in these verses…

COMMENT AND CONSIDER

Most Jewish girls in the first century were engaged to be married between the ages of 12 and 14. Engagement was defined by a written legal contract in which two extended families agreed to certain terms, including the amount of the dowry. The engaged couple continued living with their respective extended families until the time of the marriage, usually about a year later, and were expected to abstain from sexual relations. If the engagement was broken, it was considered a "divorce," and infidelity would be treated as adultery.

Luke describes a second dramatic visitation by the angel Gabriel six months after his appearance to Elizabeth, in which he delivered an even more incredible message. He told Mary she would miraculously conceive a son, although she was still a virgin, and that son would be the Messiah who would establish and rule an eternal Kingdom! Like Zechariah, Mary was shaken by this angelic visitation and was likewise reassured by Gabriel. However, it was not just the glorious appearance of an angel that troubled Mary, but also the dreadful implications of his message.

First, the obvious question was how Mary could become pregnant if she had never had sex. Second, if she did become pregnant before she and Joseph were married, it would be disastrous for her and her family. In the honor/shame culture of the first-century Middle East, your primary obligation was to bring honor to your family and to avoid bringing them shame. Mary becoming pregnant outside of marriage would bring public shame on her extended family. Since Joseph would know the child was not his, he would surely divorce her for infidelity. This calamity would ruin any chance Mary had of future marriage prospects. All her dreams for a future family were about to be shattered. Moreover, the Law prescribed death by stoning for those guilty of infidelity, and Mary would certainly be accused of this. While Gabriel's message to Zechariah was wonderfully good news, it is hard to imagine worse news for Mary to receive.

At first glance, Mary's reply to Gabriel sounds similar to Zechariah's question: *"How can this be…?"* But Gabriel's very different responses to each of them tell us the intent behind Mary's question was quite different. Zechariah was struck mute because his question was an expression of stubborn disbelief. However, instead of rebuking Mary as he did Zechariah, Gabriel answered her question, explaining the Holy Spirit would cause this miracle to take place. He offered her further promises and pointed to the testimony of Elizabeth in order to help her believe those promises. All this tells us Mary's question was not a cynical expression of stubborn disbelief but was a genuine effort to understand in order to believe.

Do you question God's promises to you? Where are your questions coming from? Are you trying to avoid the challenge of believing and living into those promises? Or are you genuinely asking for help in order to believe and trust God's promises?

Mary listened to Gabriel's response and, knowing full well all it would cost her, she chose to submit and trust God's promise, *"See, I am the Lord's servant. May it happen to me as you have said."* The result was the redemption of all creation! What might happen in your life if you do the same?

Reflect and Respond

What is Jesus saying to me right now?

What step of faith is Jesus calling me to take today?

DAY 4

READ AND LISTEN: LUKE 1:39-45

Take a minute to listen for what the Spirit is saying in these verses…

COMMENT AND CONSIDER

Elizabeth came from a priestly family and was related to Mary's family, although we don't know exactly how. Since Elizabeth was at least a generation older than Mary, she may have been her aunt or even a great aunt. Luke tells us Joseph and Mary brought their family from Nazareth to Jerusalem every year for the celebration of Passover, so these two families must have gathered together to celebrate at least once a year. (See Luke 2:41.) Perhaps this visit during their pregnancies first cemented the bond between them which would continue in the years to come.

Mary would never dare to take this rigorous five-day journey alone, so she must have joined a group of people she knew from Nazareth who were traveling to Jerusalem, either for trade or to celebrate a religious festival. Gabriel had told Mary of Elizabeth's miraculous conception, and it is understandable that Mary would want to go and talk to her about the amazing things they were both experiencing.

We can just imagine the powerful emotions this young girl must have felt after this arduous journey brought her to Elizabeth and Zechariah's front door. She must have hoped against hope that at least one person in the world would believe her story and understand what she was going through. Luke describes the profound experience Elizabeth had when the very sound of Mary's voice provoked a joyful response from the special child inside her womb! It was at this moment she was *"filled with the Holy Spirit."*

"Filled with the Spirit" is an important phrase in Luke's Gospel and Acts. We know the Holy Spirit does not force his way into our lives, but rather stands at the door with Jesus, knocking to come in. (See Revelation 3:20.) Furthermore, we know we can resist the Spirit and quench his work in our lives. (See 1 Thessalonians 5:19 and Acts 7:51.) Being "filled with the Spirit" is what happens when we say "yes" to his presence within us and yield more control of our lives to him to do God's will. It is giving the Spirit freedom to guide and empower our lives.

When Elizabeth heard Mary's voice, the child in her womb leapt for joy, and she prophetically exclaimed, *"Blessed are you among women, and your child will be blessed! How could this happen to me, that the mother of my Lord should come to me?"* Humanly speaking, Elizabeth had no way of knowing that Mary was pregnant, much less the miraculous nature of her pregnancy. This was a prophetic insight the Holy Spirit revealed to her. Elizabeth even prophesied this baby was a King when she referred to Mary as *"the mother of my Lord."* Elizabeth's openness to receiving the Spirit and submitting to his guidance allowed her to exercise the gift of prophecy and declare the truth about the child miraculously conceived inside of Mary.

It must have been incredibly reassuring for Mary to hear this prophecy from Elizabeth and to be able to share with her the details of her extraordinary experience, which would have made most people think she was crazy! Elizabeth's words and testimony helped Mary believe what Gabriel said to her was true. As Elizabeth said of Mary, *"Blessed is she who has believed that the Lord would fulfill what he has spoken to her!"*

Are there people in your life who "get you" and support you, even when you share things that might be hard to believe? Are there people who speak into your life to help you trust God's promises? Are you learning to speak words of prophecy and faith into the lives of those who look to you for help?

REFLECT AND RESPOND
What is Jesus saying to me right now?

What step of faith is Jesus calling me to take today?

DAY 5

READ AND LISTEN: LUKE 1:46-56

Take a minute to listen for what the Spirit is saying in these verses…

COMMENT AND CONSIDER

Luke continues his description of the dramatic encounter between these two miraculously pregnant women when Mary first arrived at Elizabeth and Zechariah's home in the hill country of Judea. First Elizabeth was filled with the Spirit and cried out prophetic declarations over Mary, but now it was Mary's turn to prophesy. The incredible song of praise that poured out of Mary's soul in response to Elizabeth's prophecy demonstrates how deeply moved she was to find someone who understood her inexplicable condition and affirmed it was in fact God's blessing for her and the whole world.

This beautiful and profound song is often called "the Magnificat," based on the first word in the Latin translation of Mary's song. It has been set to music in countless languages and sung during Advent in churches all over the world for two millennia. Mary embraced the universal implications of the child she carried by declaring that *"all generations will call me blessed."* Perhaps no woman has been as widely revered and honored in all of human history as Mary of Nazareth.

At the same time, Mary recognized how unlikely she was to be honored in this way. *"My soul magnifies the Lord, and my spirit rejoices in God my Savior, because he has looked with favor on the humble condition of his servant."* She was, after all, simply a young girl from a small village in rural Galilee with no particular wealth, power, or position, and yet God chose her to be the means by which he would enter his creation to redeem all of humanity and renew all of creation. Surely there can be no greater reversal of honor and power than that!

God scatters the proud, topples kings from their thrones, and leaves the rich empty. At the same time, he lifts the lowly, satisfies the hungry, and shows favor to his humble servant. This paradoxical reversal of the powerless over the powerful is one of the characteristics of the Kingdom which Mary's Son would one day proclaim and demonstrate by his scathing criticism of the hypocrisy of those in power and his open-armed welcome of the outcasts, the unclean, and sinners. Mary was prophesying the nature of her Son's coming Kingdom!

Mary recognized the child she carried was the fulfilment of God's covenant with Abraham, who was promised as many descendants as the stars of the sky, with the mandate that they would be a blessing to all the families of the earth. The exclusivism and entitlement of the Jewish religious leaders contradicted this calling to reach every tribe and nation, but the coming Messiah would call Israel back to her original mission by sending his disciples to the very ends of the earth. Again, Mary foretold the path her son would soon walk.

Jesus often described the paradoxical reversal of God's Kingdom in which the first will be last and the last first, where adults have to become like little children, and where disciples are called to take up their cross. Mary's story embodies this reversal of fortune, and her magnificent song declares that this is the surprising way God's reign works.

Where do you fit in Mary's song? Do you operate according to the hierarchical value system of the kingdoms of this world, deferring to those in positions of temporal power and position? Or do you see every person as a bearer of the divine image and worthy of honor and respect? Are you participating in the dismantling of coercive systems of oppressive power by lifting the lowly and empowering people to do the will of God? Mary was part of the great Kingdom reversal, and her Son calls us to follow her example and his.

Reflect and Respond

What is Jesus saying to me right now?

What step of faith is Jesus calling me to take today?

DAY 6

READ AND LISTEN: LUKE 1:57-66

Take a minute to listen for what the Spirit is saying in these verses…

COMMENT AND CONSIDER

In an honor/shame culture where having a large extended family was considered the highest value, childlessness was one of the deepest kinds of shame a woman could endure. The inability to conceive was considered a curse from God and was assumed to be the result of egregious sin on the part of the couple or their parents. Year after year childless Elizabeth and Zechariah had suffered the insensitive questions, unkind comments, and judgmental distancing from their neighbors. Their extended family may have been deeply disappointed because they could not contribute to the strength of their household, nor could they help assure the long-term financial success of the family business.

But when Zechariah came face to face with the angel Gabriel and stumbled out of the Temple unable to speak, everything changed. Once Elizabeth confirmed she was pregnant, word would have begun to spread in their village about this miracle, although she kept it as private as she could. Their shame was lifted! Elizabeth and Zechariah were going to have a child in their old age! Then the promise was fulfilled, and Elizabeth gave birth to a healthy baby boy.

The birth of a child in first-century Jewish culture was always a cause for celebration, particularly the birth of a son who would contribute to the family business and carry on the family name. But the birth of a son to an elderly couple was cause for extraordinary celebration by not only the extended family, but the entire community. The Law prescribed that every Hebrew male be circumcised on the eighth day following his birth. (See Genesis 17:9–14; Leviticus 12:3.) In the first century, the head of the extended family normally performed the circumcision; in this case it was probably Zechariah. Circumcision was the physical sign of the child's inclusion in God's covenant community.

Typically, the firstborn son was named after his grandfather on his father's side, or perhaps the other grandfather or even the father. When Elizabeth announced at the circumcision that the boy's name was John, it was so unusual that everyone asked Zechariah to confirm this decision. In obedience to Gabriel's command, Zechariah boldly inscribed on a wax tablet, *"His name is John."* At that very moment Zechariah regained his speech and began giving praise to God! It is hard to imagine the joy Zechariah and Elizabeth felt after all those years of disappointment and shame. Now they recognized God's intervention in their painful circumstances, and they felt the fullness of his blessing.

The miraculous nature of all these events was not lost on the people of their village and surrounding region. When the people saw Zechariah regain his speech in such a dramatic fashion, they were in awe of what God was doing and realized there was something significant about this baby boy. Who would he grow up to become? What was God's purpose for him? In biblical imagery God's hand is either with you in protection and power, or against you in opposition and judgment. It was clear to everyone that God's hand was *with* this special little boy.

Have you ever prayed for something with all your heart, only to be deeply disappointed? Do you know what it is like to be publicly shamed because you didn't meet certain social expectations? Have you ever felt afraid to believe that God might have something better in store for you? Take a moment to imagine the joy that Elizabeth and Zechariah felt in this time of God's blessing. How does their experience deepen your faith that God is good, that he is always for you regardless of your circumstances, and that his hand is with you even now? What do you want to ask God to do in your life right now? Keep asking, seeking, and knocking, and he will answer in due time.

Reflect and Respond

What is Jesus saying to me right now?

What step of faith is Jesus calling me to take today?

Footsteps Every Week: Review

Write a brief summary of what Jesus said to you each day this past week and the step of faith he called you to take:

Monday

Tuesday

Wednesday

Thursday

Friday

Saturday

Footsteps Every Week: Reflect

Big Picture

As you look over what Jesus has said to you this past week, do you see any themes? What is the most important thing you need to remember and believe?

Predictable Pattern

As you look over what Jesus called you to do this past week, is there a new predictable pattern he is inviting you to establish in your life with God and others?

Plant the Word

As you look over the readings from this past week, write out the passage that feels most important for you and memorize it over the next week:

DAY 7

READ AND LISTEN: LUKE 1:67-80
Take a minute to listen for what the Spirit is saying in these verses…

COMMENT AND CONSIDER

Like his wife Elizabeth before him, now Zechariah was *"filled with the Spirit."* This is Luke's way of saying that Zechariah relinquished more control of his life to God by surrendering to the guidance and empowerment of God's Spirit at work within and through him. From this place of surrender to the Spirit, Zechariah began to prophesy. Since the time of the prophet Malachi around 430 BC, the prophets of Israel had fallen silent. But just over 400 years later, the Spirit began stirring his people again, and the gift of prophecy was rekindled in the hearts of God's people!

Zechariah's prophecy declared that the birth of John heralded a new season of redemption and salvation that God was bringing to his people. Zechariah's language sounds very similar to the many Messianic Psalms that simultaneously celebrated God's redemptive work and promised the coming of God's anointed king, the Messiah. God promised David, *"I will raise up after you your descendant, who will come from your body, and I will establish his kingdom. He is the one who will build a house for my name, and I will establish the throne of his kingdom forever. I will be his father, and he will be my son."* (2 Samuel 7:12-14)

Zechariah pointed to the impending birth of Jesus as the fulfillment of this ancient prophecy when he declared, *"He has raised up a horn of salvation for us in the house of his servant David."* In biblical imagery a horn represented strength, because horned animals were often fearsome and dangerous. Zechariah prophesied that Jesus was this descendant of King David who would be born the Son of God and would come to establish God's eternal Kingdom and save God's people!

Then Zechariah's prophecy turned to his newborn son John, who would become a *"a prophet of the Most High"* and would *"go before the Lord to prepare his way."* This is reminiscent of the promise God gave through the last Old Testament prophet Malachi, *"See, I am going to send my messenger, and he will clear the way before me."* (Malachi 3:1) His father was foretelling that John would prepare God's people to receive the coming Messiah by pointing them toward his gift of salvation and the forgiveness of sins. Of course, this is exactly what John would grow up to do!

Luke concludes his account of John's birth with a summary of his early years growing into adulthood, *"The child grew up and became strong in spirit, and he was in the wilderness until the day of his public appearance to Israel."* Given the many parallels between John and the community of Essenes who lived at Qumran on the northwest shore of the Dead Sea, it is possible that John became a part of that community for a period of time before he began preaching and baptizing in the nearby Jordan River. Did John's elderly parents die while he was still young? Was the boy John adopted by the Qumran community as they so often did? Was it from that community of Essenes that John launched his public ministry?

We may never know the answers to these tantalizing questions, but we can be certain that what Zechariah prophesied about both John and his soon-to-be-born cousin Jesus did in fact come true. Zechariah got it right! Are you filled with the Spirit like Elizabeth and Zechariah? What would it look like for you to surrender more control of your life to the leading and empowerment of God's Spirit? Are you open to hearing what God might want to say through you to others? Are you willing to share the words and images God puts on your heart?

REFLECT AND RESPOND

What is Jesus saying to me right now?

What step of faith is Jesus calling me to take today?

DAY 8

READ AND LISTEN: LUKE 2:1-7

Take a minute to listen for what the Spirit is saying in these verses…

COMMENT AND CONSIDER

Luke anchors the birth of Jesus in the real world by telling us he was born during a Roman census ordered by Caesar Augustus, when Quirinius was governor of Syria. Augustus ruled the Empire from 27 BC to AD 14, establishing Rome as the superpower of the Mediterranean world. The strategy of the Roman Empire was to conquer new territory so they could subjugate the people and then keep them productive in order to heavily tax them. They sent the extorted money and goods back to Rome over the efficient system of roads and sea routes they had established, enriching the coffers of the Roman aristocracy. The Romans carried out regular censuses to determine how much each province should be paying in taxes each year. Typically, a Roman census was carried out at least every ten years.

We don't have an explicit record of a census at the time of Jesus' birth, but there is a record of Quirinius carrying out a census about ten years later (see Acts 5:37), which fits Luke's description of this as the *"first registration."* Some scholars have questioned Luke's assertion that people had to return to their hometown to be registered for the Roman census, but a first-century papyrus from Roman Egypt has recently come to light that reads, "Gaius Vibius Maximus, Prefect of Egypt, declares: The census by household has begun and it is accordingly necessary that all persons who are not resident at home for one reason or another at this time return to their homeplaces in order to undergo the usual registration formalities."

This is exactly why Joseph and Mary made the challenging 100-mile journey south to his ancestral hometown, unaware they were fulfilling the ancient prophecy that the Messiah would be born in Bethlehem. (See Micah 5:2.) Our typical modern western retelling of the Christmas story imagines that all the motel rooms in Bethlehem were full, so the young couple was turned away by a cruel innkeeper and forced to seek shelter in an anonymous barn where Mary gave birth to Jesus and laid him in a manger. However, culturally we know they would have gone to the extended family home of Joseph's relatives, who were culturally obligated to offer hospitality to the vulnerable couple, especially because Mary was pregnant.

Luke 2:7 is normally translated into English *"she laid him in a manger because there was no room for them in the inn."* The Greek word translated *"inn"* is *kataluma*, which describes the extra room in an extended family home that is set aside for guests or as a roadside shelter for travelers. Luke uses a different word, *pandochion*, to describe the inn where the Good Samaritan brought the wounded traveler and paid the innkeeper (*pandocheus*) to care for him (Luke 15:34-35). It is clear from the context Luke is telling us Joseph and Mary were accepted into the home of relatives in Bethlehem, but instead of offering them the guestroom as would be expected, the young couple were made to stay in that part of the home where the animals were kept. This is why Mary gave birth and laid the newborn Jesus in a manger rather than on a bed.

This puts the birth of Jesus in a new light. Why didn't they offer the guestroom to Mary? Perhaps they assumed the scandalous circumstances of Mary's pregnancy brought shame on Joseph and the family. Social expectation required that they provide shelter to their relatives, but they didn't have to honor them with the guest room. Instead, Mary and Joseph were relegated to the animal pen. As John describes Jesus' birth, he says, *"He came to his own, and his own people did not receive him."* (John 1:11)

How do cultural pressures shape your response to Jesus? Are you ashamed of him in any way? To what part of your life do you relegate Jesus? What does it mean to receive him and honor him as the true King of kings?

Reflect and Respond

What is Jesus saying to me right now?

What step of faith is Jesus calling me to take today?

DAY 9

READ AND LISTEN: LUKE 2:8-20

Take a minute to listen for what the Spirit is saying in these verses…

COMMENT AND CONSIDER

Luke describes the incredible event that took place the night Jesus was born, when the skies over Bethlehem were filled with the angelic army of God declaring the Good News of the birth of the long-awaited Messianic Savior! In the center of the modern city of Bethlehem stands the Church of the Nativity, one of the oldest continuously operating churches in the world. The altar of the church sits directly over an ancient cave which tradition tells us was the place of Jesus' birth.

It is true many first-century homes in the region were built onto the front of existing caves or rooms dug into a hillside, so this could have been a back room of Joseph's extended family home where they kept the animals at night. Furthermore, there is historical evidence that the Roman Emperor Hadrian planted a pagan worship grove dedicated to the god Tammuz over this cave in the second century, confirming it was already considered a religious site just 100 years after the time of Jesus and adding to the probability that this is the actual place of Jesus' birth.

Outside of Bethlehem is the area traditionally identified as the fields where the shepherds were keeping watch over their flocks on the night when the angel of the Lord announced the Good News of Jesus' birth. In a generally arid and barren region, Middle Eastern shepherds have to take their flocks out each day to find water and pasture, and then return to keep the sheep and goats for the night in their own home pen. But during the drier summer and fall months, they have to go further afield to find feed for the flock and so are forced to keep their flocks out in the open country at night, finding shelter in caves and crude animal pens for weeks or months at a time. This is why these shepherds were out in the open watching over their flocks by night.

The image of shepherds in the Old Testament was often applied to God and the leaders of Israel and was particularly associated with King David.

In fact, in these very fields outside of Bethlehem the young David watched over his family's flocks of sheep and goats. And yet, shepherding was considered one of the lowest vocations in the social order because it was so all-consuming, taking people away from their families for such lengths of time. Also, the Pharisees' obsession with the minutiae of their religious traditions led them to label shepherds "unclean," assuming there was no way they could keep all the ceremonial rules and purity rituals while they were watching their flocks day and night.

It is both fitting and shocking that God would choose lowly shepherds out in the fields, considered religiously unclean by some, to be the first people to receive and share the Good News of Jesus' birth. On one hand, it was shocking because these people could not regularly attend services in the synagogue, nor were they able to follow all of the ritual washings and ceremonies prescribed by the rabbis. Imagine if a long-range truck driver was the one chosen to stand on the balcony of Saint Peter's Basilica in Rome and announce the election of a new Pope!

On the other hand, it was incredibly fitting that these men who did exactly what King David used to do, in the very place where he used to do it, were the first ones to hear and declare that the promise God made to David so long ago was now fulfilled in the birth of Jesus! It fits perfectly with the pattern of God choosing a young, unmarried, peasant girl from an obscure village, who became pregnant in questionable circumstances, and was forced to give birth in an animal pen to be the one through whom this promise was fulfilled!

Are you prepared to set aside your religious assumptions and be open to God working through people you would never expect? Are you willing to respond as the shepherds did when God gives you Good News to share?

REFLECT AND RESPOND

What is Jesus saying to me right now?

What step of faith is Jesus calling me to take today?

DAY 10

READ AND LISTEN: LUKE 2:21-40

Take a minute to listen for what the Spirit is saying in these verses…

COMMENT AND CONSIDER

Like his cousin John, Jesus was circumcised on the eighth day after his birth as prescribed by the Law, and was given the name chosen for him by an angel. Jesus, "Yeshua" in Hebrew and translated "Joshua" in the Old Testament, means "God saves."

Leviticus 12:1-8 stipulates that a woman observe 40 days of isolation after her birth and then present an offering at the Temple for her purification. Exodus 13:2 commands the dedication of first-born sons to God. And so, forty days after Jesus' birth, Mary and Joseph took their newborn son on the four-mile journey north to Jerusalem and visited the great Temple complex which was newly expanded and renovated by Herod the Great. There they took immersion baths for ritual cleansing, ascended the underground stairway to the Temple courts, entered the inner courts of the Temple itself, paid the five-shekel redemption price, and offered two birds which the priests then sacrificed on the great open-air altar.

In the midst of this religious ritual, Luke introduces another figure who was filled with the Holy Spirit. Simeon was in covenant relationship with God *("righteous")*, lived according to God's will (*"devout"*), was open to direct revelation from God, and was led by the Spirit. He lived with the expectation that God was going to fulfill his promises, and God had told him he would live to see the coming of the Messiah. One morning the Holy Spirit told Simeon to go into the Temple courts and wait. When he saw Mary and Joseph with their baby fulfilling these religious requirements, he knew this was the Messiah! He took the child in his arms and began to praise God for the fulfillment of his promise.

We don't know how old Simeon was, but we get the feeling he had been waiting a long time for the fulfillment of God's promise and that now, holding this special child, he felt he had completed his purpose in life. Just as Isaiah had prophesied some 700 years before (see Isaiah 42:6-7 and 49:6), Simeon now confirmed that this child would bring light and life to all the people of the earth—both Jews and Gentiles! He went on to prophesy that Jesus would be the cause of great social reversals, that he would evoke tremendous opposition, and that Mary herself would experience the sharp pain in her heart of profound loss. As if all this were not enough, an elderly (over 100 years old!) prophetess named Anna appeared to add her confirmation that this child was born for the redemption of Jerusalem!

Starting with the angelic visitations they both had received, confirmed by the prophecies of Elizabeth and Zechariah, and followed by the joyful testimony of shepherds, now Mary and Joseph heard two more prophetic declarations that their son was, in fact, the long-awaited son of David who had come to establish an eternal Kingdom and save all God's people, both Jews and Gentiles alike! In the coming months, some exotic visitors from the east would arrive bearing expensive royal gifts, testifying about a celestial phenomenon that led them to their house and declared the birth of a great king!

It is hard to imagine more convincing proof that this child was the Messiah, yet in the years to come as Jesus grew into a man, these experiences must have come to feel like a distant dream. When Jesus began to fulfill these prophecies in his public ministry, it was difficult for Mary to accept Jesus' vision of God's Kingdom made up of both Jews and Gentiles. She came to believe her son had gone crazy, and it wasn't until he was hanging on a cross that she came to fully accept and believe in Jesus and his mission.

What things has God done to show you his purpose in your life? Have those become a distant memory, easy to forget or dismiss? What can you learn from Mary's experience?

Reflect and Respond

What is Jesus saying to me right now?

What step of faith is Jesus calling me to take today?

DAY 11

READ AND LISTEN: LUKE 2:41-52

Take a minute to listen for what the Spirit is saying in these verses…

COMMENT AND CONSIDER

Matthew tells us about the Magi from the east who made their dramatic visit to the home of Joseph's family in Bethlehem. He tells us about the angelic dream that directed Joseph to take his family away from the murderous Herod to Egypt, and then directed them back to Nazareth where Jesus could grow up in the anonymous protection of the backwaters of Galilee. (See Matthew 2:1-23.)

Archaeology has confirmed first-century Nazareth was a small village made up of observant religious Jews. Amazingly, the remains of the extended family house where Mary grew up, as well as the house of Joseph's family where she and Joseph raised Jesus and his siblings, have survived to this day! In this house and on these streets Jesus *"grew up and became strong, filled with wisdom, and God's grace was on him."* Modern Nazareth is now the largest Arab city in Israel, and it is very difficult to excavate there, so the first-century synagogue where Jesus went to primary school has yet to be found. But extensive excavations have been carried out at the nearby city of Sepphoris, which experienced a building boom during Jesus' childhood. Almost certainly this is where Jesus' family carried out their building business.

Luke tells us Jesus' family was quite devout in their religious observances, even to the point of making the two-week trip to Jerusalem and back for the Passover every year, including the year he turned twelve. At this age Jesus would have completed his basic education with the rabbis at the synagogue (called *beth sefer*, meaning "house of the book"). At 13, Jewish boys were considered men in terms of observance of the Law, and they typically began their apprenticeship into the family business.

After participating in the eight-day Passover festival with their extended family and friends in Jerusalem, Joseph and Mary began the five-day journey back to Nazareth. That night they realized with horror that Jesus was not with the relatives as they had supposed. Rushing back to Jerusalem, they spent the following day searching for the boy in vain, until finally on the third day they found him engaging in theological dialogue with the leading rabbis in the shade of the porticoes on the huge plaza that surrounded the Temple.

In typical rabbinical style, Jesus asked questions, and the teachers were astounded by his understanding and his answers. Jesus' parents were likewise astonished, not because of the profound insight and wisdom he was displaying, but because they could not comprehend why he would put them through the trauma of thinking something had happened to him. Jesus responded with an idiomatic phrase that can be translated, *"Didn't you know that it was necessary for me to be in my Father's house?"* or *"Didn't you know that it was necessary for me to be about my Father's business?"*

At age 12 Jesus understood who he was and what his mission was. He knew God was his Father and that he was called to carry out the family business of making all things new. However, his parents did not understand him or his mission. So, Jesus did something extraordinary, especially for a 12-year-old. He chose to submit to them even though they didn't get it. He chose to return to Nazareth and work as a builder, the business of his earthly family, carrying rocks and cutting stone for the next 18 years, waiting until the time was right to launch his public mission.

Are you willing to submit to others and wait for the right time to step into God's calling? Do you tend to lag behind the Spirit or rush ahead of the Spirit? What can you learn from the 12-year-old Jesus?

REFLECT AND RESPOND

What is Jesus saying to me right now?

What step of faith is Jesus calling me to take today?

DAY 12

READ AND LISTEN: LUKE 3:1-20

Take a minute to listen for what the Spirit is saying in these verses...

COMMENT AND CONSIDER

Luke continues to emphasize the historical reality of the events he records by listing the men who ruled at the time John launched his ministry in the desert. Tiberius Caesar officially began his rule in AD 14 at the death of his stepfather Augustus, but in anticipation of the transition, the elder Emperor made Tiberius co-regent in AD 11 or 12. Luke was most likely counting from the date Tiberias began his official rule, AD 14, which means John launched his ministry sometime in AD 28.

Luke describes John's inspiration with the phrase, *"God's word came to him,"* the exact phrase used to describe the call of many biblical prophets. While we have already seen the Holy Spirit awakening the gift of prophecy in everyday men and women, now in John we see the office of prophet reinstated as he stepped into a full-time ministry of preaching and baptizing. John's mission statement came from Isaiah 40: *"A voice of one crying out in the wilderness: Prepare the way for the Lord; make his paths straight!"* This is the same passage used by the Essenes at nearby Qumran, on the northwest shore of the Dead Sea, to describe their mission of preparing for the coming of what they believed would be two rulers, a priestly Messiah and a royal Messiah.

Since these Essenes focused on ritual immersion baths, lived an ascetic lifestyle in the desert, and generally chose not to marry, it is easy to see the parallels with John. However, we can also see profound contrasts. The Essenes at Qumran were obsessive about external ritual observances, but John called people to repentance, a genuine reorientation of their heart and mind. While the Essenes practiced a radical withdrawal from the world, John engaged people of every background, even tax collectors and soldiers. Although the community at Qumran expected two Messiahs, John only anticipated one. It could be that John was once part of the Essene community at Qumran but parted ways with them over these differences.

We can see clear continuity between the teaching of John and the teaching of Jesus. John was fiercely critical of those who came for baptism simply to cover their bases and not because they were ready for a real change in their lives. He called those with such false motives *"a brood of vipers,"* the very term Jesus later used for the Pharisees. He introduced the image of bearing good fruit that matched their words, which became a major theme in Jesus' teaching as well. Like Jesus, John told them that unfruitful trees would be *"cut down and thrown into the fire."* (See John 15:6.) Despite the high challenge John brought people through his teaching, like Jesus's message, John's message was described as *"good news."*

Given these parallels it is not surprising that some wondered if John was the Messiah for which they had been waiting. John was adamant in stating he was not the Anointed One and was unworthy even to untie the Messiah's sandals. John pointed out that while he was only able to immerse his followers in water as an outward symbol of their inward repentance, the One who was coming would immerse them in the very fire of God's Spirit who would transform them from the inside out!

Often, we assume that the word "repent" simply means to feel sorry for our sins. In fact, it describes a profound change of perspective that comes from hearing the Word of God and leads us to respond in concrete steps of faith. Jesus announced his ministry by declaring *"The time is fulfilled, and the kingdom of God has come near. Repent and believe the good news!"* (Mark 1:15) God's word came upon John, and he responded by boldly preaching and baptizing in preparation for Jesus' coming. How is the Word of God reorienting your perspective? What step of faith is God calling you to take? How can you prepare the way for people to receive Jesus?

Reflect and Respond
What is Jesus saying to me right now?

What step of faith is Jesus calling me to take today?

Footsteps Every Week: Review

Write a brief summary of what Jesus said to you each day this past week and the step of faith he called you to take:

Monday

Tuesday

Wednesday

Thursday

Friday

Saturday

Footsteps Every Week: Reflect

Big Picture
As you look over what Jesus has said to you this past week, do you see any themes? What is the most important thing you need to remember and believe?

Predictable Pattern
As you look over what Jesus called you to do this past week, is there a new predictable pattern he is inviting you to establish in your life with God and others?

Plant the Word
As you look over the readings from this past week, write out the passage that feels most important for you and memorize it over the next week:

DAY 13

READ AND LISTEN: LUKE 3:21-38

Take a minute to listen for what the Spirit is saying in these verses…

COMMENT AND CONSIDER

Luke is the only Gospel writer who approximates Jesus' age when he began his ministry, *"about thirty years old."* In the ancient world, 30 was considered the age of maturity when a person was ready to enter public service. Priests began their duties at the Temple when they turned 30 (Numbers 4:3), Joseph entered Pharaoh's service at 30 (Genesis 41:46), and Ezekiel was called to prophesy when he was 30 years old (Ezekiel 1:1). Most importantly for Jesus' Messianic identity, David began to rule as king when he turned 30 (2 Samuel 5:4).

Luke also roots Jesus firmly in his heritage as a Jewish descendant of David by listing his genealogy. In ancient Judaism genealogies were an important record of a person's inheritance, familial legitimacy, and legal rights. The most important of Jesus' ancestors was David, because the Messiah is the promised descendant of the greatest of Israel's kings. However, it is also significant that Luke takes Jesus' lineage not just back to Abraham, but all the way back to Noah and ultimately to Adam. Luke, the only Gentile author in the Bible, wants to remind us Jesus came to gather all of humanity, both Jews and Gentiles, into one family of God.

We might expect the Messiah to make his first appearance on the Mount of Olives, in the Temple Courts, or even in the huge palace that Herod built on the western edge of Jerusalem. Instead, Jesus chose to launch his public ministry by going out to the desert, just north of the Dead Sea, where his cousin John was baptizing people in the Jordan River. The spot on the river where John chose to preach and baptize, just to the east of Jericho, was traditionally identified as the place where Joshua had led the people of Israel through the waters of the Jordan and into the Promised Land. It was clear that John was regathering the tribes of Israel so the Messiah could lead them into a new era of promise and fruitfulness.

As Jesus came out of the water, the Holy Spirit was visibly manifested in a white form that descended from the sky and alighted on his head, reminiscent of the white doves that still inhabit that area today. Then a voice from heaven spoke over Jesus, *"You are my beloved Son; with you I am well-pleased."* It is hard to imagine a more powerful demonstration of Jesus' true identity! At the very beginning of Jesus' public mission, God the Father poured out his Spirit on his beloved Son, declaring his unequivocal approval of Jesus.

Jesus did not submit to baptism because he needed to repent. He was baptized to set an example for us to follow. He was baptized so we might know his true identity and so we might discover, in our own baptism, who we truly are. Jesus' identity as God's beloved Son was the foundation of everything he did. The Father loved the Son and was proud of him, but not for anything he had done. After all, Jesus had yet to do anything remarkable, except impress some religious teachers when he was twelve years old. The Father was pleased with the Son just because he is his Son! The same is true of us. The Father loves you and is so proud of you, not for any of the wonderful things you have done for him, but simply because you are his.

The truest thing about you is that you are God's beloved daughter or son. This is your true identity. Nothing you will ever do can make him more pleased with you than he is right now. This is the foundation of your life. Nothing and no one can take that away from you. It is from this place of knowing you are his beloved child that the rest of your life is meant to flow. Where do you find your identity? How does that shape your life? What does your baptism mean to you?

REFLECT AND RESPOND

What is Jesus saying to me right now?

What step of faith is Jesus calling me to take today?

DAY 14

READ AND LISTEN: LUKE 4:1-13

Take a minute to listen for what the Spirit is saying in these verses…

COMMENT AND CONSIDER

Luke tells us Jesus came away from his baptism *"full of the Spirit,"* meaning he was fully submitted to the purpose and power of the Spirit who was guiding his life. We might have expected Jesus' next step to be a preaching campaign or the performance of some dramatic healings. Instead, the Spirit led Jesus into the harsh desert wilderness that lay to the west of the Jordan River for a time of fasting and prayer. There he prepared for the spiritual battle that lay ahead.

A deep valley called Wadi Qelt flows out of the desert hills into the Jordan rift valley, just southwest of Jericho. It is unique because it contains three large springs that provide water in an otherwise barren region. Herod the Great built his winter palace on the outskirts of Jericho at the mouth of Wadi Qelt and constructed two aqueducts that brought water from those springs to his palace, which we can still see today. This is almost certainly the area where Jesus spent his forty days and nights in the wilderness, because although he was fasting from food, he would have needed a source of water, which was uniquely available in this valley.

Fasting is a spiritual discipline that brings us to a deeper knowledge of how dependent on God we are for everything. The Spirit led Jesus to this barren place for a time of preparation so he would be able to carry out his mission, not in his own strength and knowledge, but in the power and wisdom of his Father. When Jesus was physically at his weakest, the devil came to him, unaware this was actually Jesus' point of greatest strength because he was relying completely on the authority and power given to him by his Father the King.

Notice how the tempter began his attack: *"If you are the Son of God, tell this stone to become bread."* The devil will always tempt you to question your identity, because he knows if he can undermine who you are, he can keep you from doing what you are meant to do. But Jesus was deeply rooted in his identity as the beloved Son and so responded not in his own wisdom and strength, but as a representative of his Father the King. *"It is written: Man must not live on bread alone."* Jesus didn't speak his own words, but rather the words the Father had given him to speak. We have been authorized by Jesus, just as he was by his Father, to speak and act on behalf of our Father the King. When we exercise this kind of authority by faith, the power of the Spirit flows through us just as it flowed through Jesus!

The devil appealed to Jesus' appetite, exaggerated as it was from forty days of fasting, and he will do the same to us. But, exercising the authority of his Father the King, Jesus overcame the attack of the enemy by the power of the Spirit. The devil attacked two more times, appealing to Jesus' ambition and his desire for approval, but again Jesus responded as an authorized representative of his Father the King, *"It is written…"* Each time Jesus exercised the authority given to him to represent his Father the King, the power of the Spirit flowed through him to overcome the deceiver. The same is true for us.

If you have decided to follow Jesus, you have joined the movement of his coming Kingdom in which God's will is done on earth as it is in heaven. This will bring you into direct conflict with the devil and his kingdom of darkness. The only way you will be able to fulfill your calling in God's Kingdom is if you learn to fight these kinds of spiritual battles and win. Have you claimed your identity as a son or daughter of the King? Do you believe you have been authorized to represent him by speaking and acting on his behalf? Are you learning to let the power of the Spirit flow through you to do God's will?

REFLECT AND RESPOND

What is Jesus saying to me right now?

What step of faith is Jesus calling me to take today?

DAY 15

READ AND LISTEN: LUKE 4:14-30

Take a minute to listen for what the Spirit is saying in these verses...

COMMENT AND CONSIDER

In his baptism Jesus was filled with the Holy Spirit, who then led him into the desert for a time of fasting, prayer, and testing by the devil. Jesus defeated the devil and came out of this battle to return to Galilee *"in the power of the Spirit."* According to the other Gospels, Jesus preached with authority in various synagogues along the way and attended a wedding at Cana, but Luke makes it clear Jesus was ultimately returning to his hometown of Nazareth.

It is easy for those of us who are shaped by modern western culture to read the Bible through an individualistic lens. We tend to see people as solo agents, independent from those around them. However, in the biblical world people always understood themselves and others in the context of a network of relationships in their extended family and community. So, we must remember Jesus was not just returning to his geographical hometown, but also coming back to his extended family, which was the primary way he would be defined. Culturally, it makes the most sense to assume Jesus was returning to invite his extended family to join him in his Kingdom calling and to make his extended family home the headquarters of his new mission.

When Jesus arrived in Nazareth, he did not check into a local motel but likely stayed in that extended family home, the remains of which are still visible today. When Jesus went to the synagogue that Saturday morning, he was not going by himself as a modern individual, but with his extended family. Although he was not formally trained as a rabbi, reports of the authority and power of Jesus' teaching had already come to the leaders of the synagogue in Nazareth, so they invited this hometown builder to teach from the Scriptures. When Jesus read Isaiah's famous description of the Messianic jubilee (Isaiah 61:1-2), everyone in the synagogue was filled with expectation. What would Jesus say about this long-awaited promise of the Anointed King who would come to make everything right again?

When Jesus sat down on the Moses Seat, the place from which rabbis taught in the synagogue, every eye was fixed on him. When he finally spoke and said, *"Today as you listen, this Scripture has been fulfilled,"* there must have been a collective gasp from the crowd. For centuries they had endured the occupation and oppression of the Assyrians, Babylonians, Persians, Greeks, and now the Romans. They were filled with a deep hatred for the pagan Gentiles who had oppressed them for so long, had developed a sense of religious entitlement as God's chosen people, and were longing for the fulfillment of this promise. If Jesus had just ended his message there, he would have been the most popular guy in Nazareth!

Jesus went on to tell the stories of the widow from Zarephath and Naaman the Syrian, both of whom were Gentiles God chose to bless. (See 1 Kings 17 and 2 Kings 5.) Jesus' point was clear to everyone there: the Good News of the Kingdom of God is not just for Jews, it is for everyone, even Gentiles! This inclusion of the Gentiles enraged the deeply embittered crowd, and they dragged Jesus out to a nearby cliff, preparing to stone him for blasphemy and heresy. Jesus' brothers and cousins did not stand up to defend him. Not even his own mother spoke for him. There could be no more complete act of rejection than this. As Jesus said, *"A prophet is not without honor except in his hometown, among his relatives, and in his household."* (Mark 6:4)

How do you respond when you read a saying of Jesus that contradicts your assumptions? How do you feel about Jesus accepting people you believe are evil? Are you willing to be identified with Jesus even if those around you are rejecting him? Do you know how to honor Jesus by speaking on his behalf to others who don't embrace him?

Reflect and Respond
What is Jesus saying to me right now?

What step of faith is Jesus calling me to take today?

DAY 16

READ AND LISTEN: LUKE 4:31-44

Take a minute to listen for what the Spirit is saying in these verses…

COMMENT AND CONSIDER

Jesus went directly from the murderous crowd in Nazareth to Capernaum on the north shore of the Sea of Galilee, about a half day's journey. At the time of his baptism, Jesus met three disciples of John the Baptist who wanted to get to know him, so he welcomed them, listened to them, and served them. (See John 1:35-42.) All three of them, Andrew, Simon, and (probably) John, came from Capernaum. Now Jesus seemed to be going there to see if they would welcome him, listen to him, and serve him as well. This is a clear example of the "person of peace" principle Jesus would later teach his disciples when preparing to send them out on mission. (See Luke 10:1-12.)

Capernaum was a thriving fishing town that boasted a large basalt synagogue which, surprisingly, was paid for by a Roman centurion. (See Luke 7:5.) This synagogue has been excavated, and the black basalt foundations are still visible beneath the walls of the white limestone synagogue we see there today, built on the exact same footprint of the original a few hundred years later. Despite his lack of formal training, Jesus was invited to teach in this synagogue, and people were amazed at the authority of his words because he spoke directly as a representative of his Father. Likewise, they were amazed by the power with which he easily cast out demonic spirits.

Jesus confirmed that Simon and Andrew were people of peace to him because they invited Jesus into their home following the synagogue service. Amazingly, archaeologists have identified the house of Simon and Andrew just one block south of the synagogue, on the waterfront of Capernaum. In biblical culture people lived in extended family homes, with several nuclear families inhabiting the rooms built around a central courtyard, accessed through a single exterior door. The extended family (Greek: *oikos*) was built around a family business which was typically carried out in the courtyard of their home, an area where they also cooked their meals and shared daily life together.

In an honor/shame culture, the highest priority was building the honor of your extended family and protecting it from shame. Therefore, you only invited people into your *oikos* who would bring honor to your family, and certainly did not welcome those of low social standing or questionable moral character. The members of Simon and Andrew's extended family would have been thrilled to have Jesus in their home because hosting a famous rabbi brought honor to their family. When Jesus healed Peter's mother-in-law and they shared a meal together, their enthusiasm for Jesus only grew. However, Jesus then did something shocking which must have made them all wonder if they had made a terrible mistake. Jesus opened the door of their house and welcomed everyone into their *oikos*, even the lame and the demon-possessed!

As people filled the courtyard and the rooms of the house, Jesus taught them the Good News of the Kingdom and demonstrated that Kingdom by healing those who were broken and delivering those who were oppressed. Jesus was showing Simon and Andrew a whole new way of being a family. Normally an *oikos* existed to protect and serve the *oikos*, but Jesus was showing them how to be a family that exists for others. Not just a biological family, but a spiritual family. Not just a nuclear family, but an extended family. Not just a family that serves itself, but a family on mission!

This home became the center of Jesus' mission and the heart of the discipling culture he built. This way of sharing life and mission together became the pattern Jesus' disciples replicated in towns and cities across the Roman empire. They came to be called churches and would change the world forever.

How does this new kind of family challenge your inherited way of life? How does this pattern affect your assumptions about the definition of the church? What would it look like to live with others more intentionally the way Jesus did?

REFLECT AND RESPOND
What is Jesus saying to me right now?

What step of faith is Jesus calling me to take today?

DAY 17

READ AND LISTEN: LUKE 5:1-11

Take a minute to listen for what the Spirit is saying in these verses…

COMMENT AND CONSIDER

Simon and Andrew were part of a family fishing business on the Sea of Galilee along with the members of their extended family and their partners, Zebedee and his sons, James and John. They had welcomed Jesus into their extended family and he, in turn, invited the whole town into their home! Although it must have been disorienting for them, they were also honored to be so closely associated with this famous, if controversial, rabbi! As Jesus' fame grew, so did the crowds who came to listen to him and witness his deeds of power. Soon the crowds grew so large Jesus had to gather people on the desolate hillsides overlooking the lake outside of Capernaum. One day the large crowd pressed in on him so hard that Jesus asked Simon to row him out from the shore where he could put some distance between him and the crowd, using the reflective property of the water to carry his voice to those who sat down on the hillside.

Simon and Andrew had been fishing all night with Zebedee and his sons and their hired men. This was, and still is, the best time to fish because the fish come to the surface to feed at night, and in the darkness they are less likely to see the nets and avoid capture. However, these seasoned professional fishermen had caught nothing all night long. When Jesus asked Simon to use his boat, he was happy to help because he had become a friend of Jesus, and friends will serve you. Jesus taught the crowds from the boat, but by mid-day he had finished speaking and sent them home. Then Jesus decided to see if Simon was ready to take the next step in their relationship when he said to him, *"Put out into deep water and let down your nets for a catch."*

Simon, tired and frustrated from a fruitless night of work, must have had a visceral reaction to Jesus' words. This was terrible fishing advice! Everyone knew you should fish at night in the shallow water near the shore where your nets can stretch from the surface down to the bottom, so you can trap the fish. Who did this stonemason think he was, telling Simon how to fish? After all, he had spent his whole life fishing these waters, like his father and grandfather before him, and he had made a good living at it! And yet he had fished all night and caught nothing...

Jesus was testing Simon by giving him terrible fishing advice. A friend will serve you, but a follower will submit to you. Jesus was pressing Simon to see if he was ready to move from being his friend to becoming his follower. A disciple is willing to trust their rabbi enough to listen to his words and follow his example, even if it means going against his own instincts and experience. In that critical moment Simon made a fateful decision. *"Master,"* Simon replied, *"we've worked hard all night long and caught nothing. But if you say so, I'll let down the nets."* And then he had the catch of a lifetime! His nets were breaking, so he called his partners James and John to come help. Both boats were so full of fish they began to sink.

In the most dramatic fashion, Simon discovered his life would be so much more fruitful if he chose to submit to Jesus and follow him no matter what! Falling down at Jesus' knees in the boat, face down in the flopping fish, Simon gave himself over to Jesus and decided he would let Jesus teach him how to fish for people! Are you Jesus' friend or his follower? Do you follow your own instincts and do what you think is right, or are you submitting to Jesus and allowing him to shape and guide your life?

REFLECT AND RESPOND
What is Jesus saying to me right now?

What step of faith is Jesus calling me to take today?

DAY 18

READ AND LISTEN: LUKE 5:12-16
Take a minute to listen for what the Spirit is saying in these verses…

COMMENT AND CONSIDER

In the book of Leviticus, God gave the Jewish people a series of rules about what they could eat and not eat, touch, and not touch. These were not moral codes, but rather symbolic practices meant to remind them not to become defiled by the pagan cultures that surrounded them. God told the people through Moses, *"Be holy because I, the Lord your God, am holy."* (Leviticus 19:2) To be holy is to be special, unique, and distinct from those around you. They were to stand out from the pagan cultures that surrounded them.

In Jesus' time the Pharisees were zealous about the application of these purity laws and emphasized the need for people to separate themselves from anything or anyone identified as "impure." They went far beyond the literal meaning of the biblical purity laws, adding many more distinctions and separations to the Law itself. Skin diseases were considered one of the most extreme forms of impurity, and those considered "lepers" were required to separate themselves from family and society in general. These unfortunate souls were often forced to live together in leper colonies, wear rags, carry signs around their necks identifying them as lepers, and cry out "leper" anytime someone approached them.

Jesus followed the intent of the written biblical Law but was not bound by the complex oral traditions of the Pharisees. He was clear that impurity was not a matter of touching or eating certain things, but instead determined by the words and actions that flow from the human heart. (See Mark 7:17-23.) When Jesus reached out and touched this leper, it was a shocking act of inclusion that violated the Pharisees' abhorrence of coming anywhere close to someone or something that was obviously considered ceremonially "unclean."

This man came to Jesus in faith. *"Lord, if you are willing, you can make me clean."* Jesus responded to this bold confession of faith by expressing his desire to see the man made whole and restored to his community. As we see throughout the Gospels, Jesus did not ask the Father to heal this man, but exercised the authority given to him as a representative of his Father the King and simply commanded the leprosy to leave with immediate effect. Jesus said, "*I am willing; be made clean*," and immediately the leprosy left him. Jesus expressed love and compassion for this man who was ostracized from his family and community, physically welcoming him into the family of God. Jesus also showed us our Father wants us to be whole and well. He demonstrated the power that flows through those who exercise his authority by faith.

Jesus told the man to go and show himself to the priest and make an offering because this was what the Law required. (See Leviticus 14:1-57.) Jesus did not disregard the written Law, but he refused to be defined by the overly legalistic and harsh interpretations of the Pharisees. They believed that things and people which were unclean would make anyone who touched them unclean, and so they taught people to separate themselves from anything or anyone who might compromise their state of purity. Jesus, on the other hand, knew that in the Kingdom of God it is exactly the opposite; the clean have the power to make the unclean clean!

As Jesus demonstrated his authority and power, even over diseases that made people ceremonially unclean, his popularity grew. Rather than seek the limelight, Jesus withdrew from the crowds and drew even closer to his heavenly Father in prayer, knowing he would need strength more than ever to continue his mission in this celebrity culture.

From what people do you consciously or unconsciously distance yourself? What would it mean to touch them the way Jesus did? How can you become a conduit of God's power to bless others? What is the role of prayer in that process?

REFLECT AND RESPOND

What is Jesus saying to me right now?

What step of faith is Jesus calling me to take today?

Footsteps Every Week: Review

Write a brief summary of what Jesus said to you each day this past week and the step of faith he called you to take:

Monday

Tuesday

Wednesday

Thursday

Friday

Saturday

Footsteps Every Week: Reflect

Big Picture
As you look over what Jesus has said to you this past week, do you see any themes? What is the most important thing you need to remember and believe?

Predictable Pattern
As you look over what Jesus called you to do this past week, is there a new predictable pattern he is inviting you to establish in your life with God and others?

Plant the Word
As you look over the readings from this past week, write out the passage that feels most important for you and memorize it over the next week:

DAY 19

READ AND LISTEN: LUKE 5:17-26

Take a minute to listen for what the Spirit is saying in these verses...

COMMENT AND CONSIDER

From Matthew's and Mark's accounts, we know this healing took place in the extended family home of Simon and Andrew in Capernaum. This was the regular gathering place where Jesus invested in a houseful of disciples and welcomed the outcast and broken to experience the Kingdom of God in a spiritual family. Jesus welcomed not only those outside the religious establishment, but also the wealthy elite and the religious leaders, who were so often critical of his teaching and his ministry. These scribes and Pharisees had come from all over Israel to see for themselves this Rabbi who spoke of God's reign and demonstrated it by his life. Jesus' gracious acceptance was wide enough to span all the religious and social divides of his culture. Luke also tells us Jesus operated in the authority of the Father to do his will on earth through the supernatural power of the Spirit at work in him.

Four men had a friend who was paralyzed. They had heard testimony of Jesus' healing power and hoped that, if they could get their friend to him, he could be healed as well. When they arrived at the extended family home of Simon and Andrew, they discovered to their dismay the central courtyard of the house was completely full of people, which meant they could not get their friend to Jesus. Spotting the stone steps in the courtyard leading up to the rooftop, they came up with a crazy idea! Up the steps they went, carrying their paralyzed friend across the mud-thatched roof until they were above the main room where Jesus was teaching. Removing the protective tiles and digging through the layers of mud and straw, they made a large opening between the rafters and lowered their friend on his stretcher down to where Jesus was.

We can just imagine what Simon and Andrew were thinking about their roof being torn open—but Jesus didn't see the damage, he saw the faith of these four. He responded by saying to the paralyzed man, *"Friend, your sins are forgiven."* This was not exactly the response these four men were hoping for. It was pretty obvious to everyone what their friend's need was, but Jesus looked deeper. In the modern western world, we tend to compartmentalize the respective parts of human personality, assuming the physical has nothing to do with the mental, emotional, or spiritual aspects of who we are. In the ancient world they understood each person is an interconnected whole, where each part of us affects the others. Jesus saw that this man was not only crippled by the paralysis of his legs, but other issues held him down as well.

The religious leaders were inwardly shocked Jesus would declare the forgiveness of this man's sins with such authority. *"Who is this man who speaks blasphemies? Who can forgive sins but God alone?"* Jesus did not deny his divinity but, discerning their thoughts, he proceeded to heal this man as a demonstration that he was authorized to carry out God's will on earth as it is in heaven. The Kingdom of God is heaven breaking into earth. In heaven there is no paralysis. In heaven there is no guilt or sin or condemnation. Just as surely as they saw this paralytic stand up and walk, so they could know God was dealing with sin once and for all. After his death and resurrection, Jesus explicitly gave his disciples the authority to declare the forgiveness of sins, along with the power to heal the broken. (See Luke 9:1 and John 20:21-23.)

Knowing he would give him what their friend desperately needed, these four men were determined to do whatever it took to get him close to Jesus. What are you willing to do to bring people you care about face to face with Jesus? Are you willing to accept the authority Jesus has given you to declare the forgiveness of sins and the power of the Spirit to heal the broken?

Reflect and Respond

What is Jesus saying to me right now?

What step of faith is Jesus calling me to take today?

DAY 20

READ AND LISTEN: LUKE 5:27-39

Take a minute to listen for what the Spirit is saying in these verses…

COMMENT AND CONSIDER

The Roman Empire was the undisputed superpower controlling the Mediterranean world at the time of Jesus. By the sheer brute force of their relentless legions, they conquered lands as far west as Britain, as far south as Libya, as far north as Germania, and as far east as Mesopotamia. The primary purpose of this territorial conquest was to broaden their tax base. By controlling the lands they conquered and keeping the populations productive, they could exact exorbitant taxes, shipping the money and goods back to Rome to fill the coffers of the Roman aristocracy.

Roman governors ruled the neighboring lands directly for the Empire, but the further flung provinces were typically run by a local king or warlord who ruled on behalf of Rome. The primary job of these proxy rulers was to keep the people subdued, make sure nothing interfered with their productivity, efficiently extract the required tax revenue, and send it securely back to Rome. Heavy taxation by an occupying force was deeply resented, so the Romans typically employed members of the local community to collect the required payments. To incentivize them and make sure the quota was met each year, the Romans allowed these tax collectors to keep anything they collected above the annual levy.

Levi, whose Roman name was Matthew, was a Jewish tax collector working for the Romans near Capernaum. The Via Maris, a major trade route that connected Egypt to Mesopotamia, ran along the north shore of the Sea of Galilee and then turned north to Damascus. The border between Herod Antipas' territory and Herod Philip's territory lay just to the east of Capernaum, and the Via Maris ran directly beside Capernaum, so the Romans collected toll taxes from the countless merchants who transported their goods along that road and across that border. Levi operated the toll booth on the Via Maris to the east of Capernaum.

It is not hard to imagine how unpopular tax collectors like Levi were in Jewish society. They were considered traitors for colluding with the enemy occupiers. They were considered thieves for collecting more than the already excessive taxation. They were considered unclean for being in fellowship with pagans. It is fair to say they were the most hated group in first-century Judaism. This is what makes Jesus' decision to invite Levi the tax collector into his inner circle so outrageous. Not only the religious leaders, but also Jesus' blue-collar disciples would have been deeply angered by Jesus legitimizing such a social pariah. And then Jesus took them to spend the rest of the day eating in Levi's home with the local tax collectors and his other morally questionable friends! This would have tested the loyalty of all the disciples, particularly Simon the (former) Zealot, who at one point in his life was sworn to destroy such enemies of Israel.

The religious leaders couldn't stand by and say nothing, so they began to berate Jesus' disciples, asking them, *"Why do you eat and drink with tax collectors and sinners?"* Jesus responded with a profound image of the nature of his Kingdom: *"It is not those who are healthy who need a doctor, but those who are sick. I have not come to call the righteous, but sinners to repentance."* By calling Levi to be one of his core disciples, Jesus provocatively demonstrated the nature of his all-inclusive Kingdom mission, to seek and save the lost.

What people in your life seem the furthest from God? Do you find yourself subconsciously writing them off and assuming that they could never be part of God's family or Kingdom? How does Jesus' call of Levi challenge those assumptions? Who is Jesus calling you to invite into your life who is far from God?

Reflect and Respond

What is Jesus saying to me right now?

What step of faith is Jesus calling me to take today?

DAY 21

READ AND LISTEN: LUKE 5:33-39

Take a minute to listen for what the Spirit is saying in these verses…

COMMENT AND CONSIDER

Although fasting was only required once a year on the Day of Atonement, pious Jews in the time of Jesus typically fasted from food and strong drink twice a week on Mondays and Thursdays. The Pharisees were particularly committed to this practice and liked to make a public show of their abstinence by wearing sackcloth and going out in public with their hair unkempt and faces unwashed. (See Matthew 6:16.) John the Baptist was also known for his ascetic lifestyle, which included regular fasting and the rejection of common creature comforts. By contrast Jesus and his disciples attended festive banquets held in his honor and generally seemed to nurture a culture of celebration. On one occasion Jesus' miraculously turned water into the best wine anyone had ever tasted in order to keep a friend's wedding celebration from turning into a disaster of family shame.

In the context of Jesus' scandalous invitation for the tax collector Levi to join his inner circle of full-time disciples, some cast doubt on Jesus' religious credibility. *"John's disciples fast often and say prayers, and those of the Pharisees do the same, but yours eat and drink."* The subtext of the statement is an obvious indictment of Jesus' character based on a lack of religious rigor. Jesus' answer affirmed the validity of fasting as a spiritual discipline—after all, he fasted for forty days before launching his public ministry! But he made the point that there is an appropriate time and a season for everything, including fasting, and this was not that time.

In the first century, a Jewish wedding began with the bridegroom arriving at the extended family home of the bride with his entourage to escort the bride and her bridesmaids to the extended family home of the bridegroom. The couple recited the wedding formalities in the courtyard of the house, and then the bridegroom's family threw a lavish party! The celebration could go on for a week or more, as we still see today in traditional Arab villages in the Middle East.

If some of the guests at a wedding celebration wore torn clothes, had unwashed faces, and refused to eat, it would be interpreted as a huge insult to the hosting family and the couple being married. This is how Jesus explained his lack of emphasis on fasting. There was simply too much to celebrate! He felt a sense of urgency to train his disciples and prepare them so they would be able to continue the Kingdom movement he began. When the time came for his departure, Jesus knew they would return to a pattern of regular fasting, but for now fasting was not needed.

Then Jesus gave his disciples two vivid images to describe the unique nature of the revelation unfolding through his teaching and life. Everyone knew not to sew a patch of new cloth onto an old garment that needed mending, because the patch would shrink while the old garment stayed the same and pull out the stitches. In the same way, the revelation Jesus was bringing of the New Covenant could not simply be added to the Old Covenant.

Old and new wineskins taught a similar lesson. The hair was scraped from the hide of a sheep or goat, the edges were sewn together, and the resulting leather bag was used to store and transport wine. As the new wine fermented, it expanded, and the leather wineskin stretched to accommodate it. Once a wineskin was stretched out, it was no longer good for storing new wine, because it couldn't stretch much further. The new wine would expand and burst the wineskin. New wine needed flexible new wineskins that could accommodate its expansion. Jesus said the same was true of his teaching and demonstration of the Kingdom of God. The old could not contain the new.

We are the new wineskins that can accommodate the revolutionary nature of the new life Jesus demonstrated and communicated. Are you flexible enough to receive the new wine of Jesus' Kingdom? How do you need to be stretched in order to convey this expanded vision of how life is meant to be lived?

Reflect and Respond

What is Jesus saying to me right now?

What step of faith is Jesus calling me to take today?

DAY 22

READ AND LISTEN: LUKE 6:1-11

Take a minute to listen for what the Spirit is saying in these verses…

COMMENT AND CONSIDER

Jesus grew up in a religiously observant family who followed the Laws of Moses and participated in the traditions of Judaism. He was clear in his affirmation of the written Law of the Old Testament: *"Don't think that I came to abolish the Law or the Prophets. I did not come to abolish but to fulfill. For truly I tell you, until heaven and earth pass away, not the smallest letter or one stroke of a letter will pass away from the law until all things are accomplished."* (Matthew 5:17-18) However, he did not affirm the many additional rules and traditions the rabbis had added to the Law. He showed his followers a different way to interpret and practice the will of God revealed in the Law.

One of the laws Jesus followed was a 24-hour Sabbath period of rest each week, starting at sundown on Friday and continuing until sundown on Saturday. He understood this weekly rhythm of rest and reconnecting with the heavenly Father is a key to bearing good fruit that lasts. The Law was clear that Sabbath rest applied even during the critical season of harvest. *"You are to labor six days but you must rest on the seventh day; you must even rest during plowing and harvesting times."* (Exodus 34:21) The Pharisees took it much further, adding many additional rules including the prohibition of tying a knot or sewing two stitches.

As Jesus and his disciples passed through a grainfield on the Sabbath they plucked some heads of grain, rubbing them between their palms to loosen the husks, and ate the grains. When the Pharisees accused them of breaking the commandment prohibiting the harvest of grain on the Sabbath, Jesus recounted the time David asked Ahimelech the priest in Nob to give him five of the consecrated loaves of bread from the Tabernacle to feed his men. (See 1 Samuel 21:2-6.) This violated the law that only the priests were allowed to eat the consecrated bread, but it met a vital need of feeding David's men for battle.

Jesus' point in referencing this biblical precedent is that meeting human needs supersedes the symbolism of ceremonial laws. Obviously, rubbing some heads of grain between their hands for a snack on the Sabbath was not keeping them from enjoying the rest and renewal God offered them. Jesus pointed people back to the purpose of Sabbath, which was being hindered by the burdensome rules of the Pharisees. Exercising his authority to definitively interpret the Law, Jesus declared, *"The Son of Man is Lord of the Sabbath."*

Luke followed this dramatic event with the account of another Sabbath confrontation. Jesus was teaching in a synagogue on the Sabbath where there was a man with a paralyzed and atrophied hand. The Pharisees were ready to denounce Jesus if he healed the man, because they taught that healing on the Sabbath was only allowed "whenever there is doubt whether life is in danger." A withered hand did not rise to the level of a life-threatening emergency.

Jesus was aware of their desire to accuse him, but rather than avoid the controversy, he decided to confront their misguided interpretation of the Law directly. Calling the man to the front of the synagogue, Jesus asked these religious teachers, *"Is it lawful to do good on the Sabbath or to do evil, to save life or to destroy it?"* When they failed to answer, Jesus boldly healed the man's hand, demonstrating his own interpretation that meeting human needs supersedes religious ceremony. The religious leaders were so threatened by Jesus' powerful demonstration of his authority to correctly interpret the Law that they spent the rest of the Sabbath plotting how to get rid of Jesus. They had accused Jesus of breaking the Sabbath by saving a life, but now they broke it by plotting to destroy a life. The irony and hypocrisy could scarcely be any more obvious!

What religious traditions or customs have you seen take precedence over meeting human needs? Are you prepared to let go of familiar and comfortable practices if they keep you from doing God's will on earth as it is done in heaven?

Reflect and Respond
What is Jesus saying to me right now?

What step of faith is Jesus calling me to take today?

DAY 23

READ AND LISTEN: LUKE 6:12-26

Take a minute to listen for what the Spirit is saying in these verses…

COMMENT AND CONSIDER

As we read the Gospel accounts of Jesus' mission, we can see three distinct relational dimensions to his extraordinary life. The first dimension of Jesus' life was *upward*, his intimate relationship with the Father. He spent all night in prayer on the mountain, drawing close, pouring out his heart, and listening for the Father's voice. He spent forty days fasting and praying in the desert. He woke early in the morning to spend time alone with the Father. He lived his life in faithful response to the Father's direction, deeply rooted in his identity as a Son who was authorized to represent his Father the King. Jesus said, *"Truly I tell you, the Son is not able to do anything on his own, but only what he sees the Father doing. For whatever the Father does, the Son likewise does these things."* (John 5:19)

In that all-night vigil, Jesus prayed to discern whom he should invite into his inner circle of disciples. The second dimension of Jesus' life was *inward*, his invitation for people to draw near to him, go deeper in their relationships, and function as a spiritual family. When his biological family rejected him, he found people of peace who were interested in living as brothers and sisters. In that spiritual family, he functioned as a spiritual parent who helped each member become all they were meant to be and do all they were called to do. This was where Jesus made disciple-making disciples. Jesus prayed we would learn to draw near to him and each other the way he drew near to the Father, *"May they all be one, as you, Father, are in me and I am in you."* (John 17:21)

After identifying his twelve closest disciples, Jesus led them down the mountain onto the plain where a large crowd of people from all the surrounding regions had gathered to hear him teach and be healed of their diseases, and he healed them all. The third dimension of Jesus' life was *outward*, his determination to touch the physically and spiritually broken and reach those who were far from God. His heart was for the sheep who were without a shepherd. He went where lost people were searching for purpose and meaning. He healed the broken and delivered the oppressed. He welcomed the outcast into his spiritual family. Jesus was the Good Shepherd who was always going after the one lost sheep. He was the woman searching for the lost coin. He described his mission when he said, *"the Son of Man has come to seek and to save the lost."* (Luke 19:10)

These three dimensions of Jesus' life, up with the Father, in with the disciples, and out with the world, comprise what I like to call the Jesus-shaped life. Discipleship is the journey of growing these three relational dimensions through our relationship with those who are ahead of us on the journey. We need people in our lives who model the Way of Jesus for us and teach us the Truth of Jesus, so we can live more of the Life of Jesus. The natural outcome of this Life is that we, in turn, will do the same for others.

As Jesus promised the disciples, this journey will lead us into a deeper experience of the Kingdom of God where things operate differently than in the kingdoms of this world. This life of Jesus-shaped discipleship will produce an indestructible joy not dependent on the circumstances of this world. This abundant life is not produced by worldly riches, comforts, consumption, or recognition. Rather it is joy that endures even in the midst of poverty, hunger, weeping, rejection, and attack. This is the Kingdom of God and the eternal inheritance of all those who follow Jesus, trust his truth, and learn to live his three-dimensional life.

Which dimension of Jesus' life is lacking in your life right now? How can you grow in that area to become more like Jesus? What does it look like to base your life on the values of God's Kingdom rather than the kingdoms of this world?

REFLECT AND RESPOND
What is Jesus saying to me right now?

What step of faith is Jesus calling me to take today?

DAY 24

READ AND LISTEN: LUKE 6:27-36

Take a minute to listen for what the Spirit is saying in these verses...

COMMENT AND CONSIDER

One of Jesus' most famous collection of teachings is recorded in Matthew 5-7. It is typically called "The Sermon on the Mount" because Matthew says that Jesus *"went up on the mountain, and after he sat down, his disciples came to him. Then he began to teach them..."* (Matthew 5:1-2) But here we read similar teachings when Jesus *"stood on a level place..."* (Luke 6:17) Did Jesus give these teachings from the mountain or from the plain? Did he teach Matthew's version or Luke's version? It is easy to forget that Jesus was an itinerant teacher and traveled from village to village, demonstrating the Kingdom of God and teaching what it means. Obviously, Jesus had to repeat his core teachings over and over again in different places so people could hear them. So it makes sense that different Gospel writers would record different versions of the same basic teachings in different contexts.

In these verses Jesus calls us to a radical ethic of unconditional love for all people that is unparalleled in its challenge to the human bias toward self-interest. The word used for "love" here is the Greek verb *agapeo*, which means: a determination to act for the good of another regardless of their disposition toward you. Agape is unconditional, self-giving love. Jesus calls us to express this kind of love toward the most difficult people in our lives. Notice Jesus is not talking about warm, fuzzy feelings; he is describing concrete actions: do good to them, bless them, pray for them. This kind of love demonstrates consideration for others and recognizes their intrinsic value as fellow children of God.

In the Law it says, *"Do not show pity: life for life, eye for eye, tooth for tooth, hand for hand, and foot for foot."* (Deuteronomy 19:21) This principle of retribution, how the damage and loss that you inflict will be inflicted on you, is universal in human societies. The purpose of this retribution is to dissuade evildoers from causing damage to others, *"Then everyone else will hear and be afraid, and they will never again do anything evil like this among you."* (Deuteronomy 19:20) But Jesus shattered all these concepts of justice and reparation when he told us to offer our other cheek when struck in the face and to offer our shirt when someone steals our coat.

Some people are motivated to do good by the prospect that good will be done to them in response to their kindness toward others. However, Jesus points out this is simply a more subtle form of the sinful human impulse to serve our own self-interest. As he says, *"Even sinners love those who love them."* Jesus explains that a selfless expression of unconditional love is a reflection of the God who *"is gracious to the ungrateful and evil."* And so, we are to *"Be merciful, just as your Father also is merciful."* Mercy is withholding the retribution that we deserve. Grace is offering the goodwill that we don't deserve. God lavishes both on us without limit!

Such a challenging ethic of unconditional love and forgiveness seems impossible from a human point of view, until we are reminded this is the very grace and love God shows to us every single day. Jesus told a parable of a hypocritical man who refused to forgive the relatively small debt owed to him immediately after he had been forgiven an impossibly huge sum. (See Matthew 18:21-35.) When we recognize and receive the incomparable grace and mercy of God toward us, we find the Source of unconditional love who empowers us to freely give to others in love, even those who refuse to love us in return.

Who is the person to whom God is calling you to demonstrate his unconditional love today? Who is the person from whom God is calling you to withhold retribution and extend mercy instead today?

REFLECT AND RESPOND

What is Jesus saying to me right now?

What step of faith is Jesus calling me to take today?

Footsteps Every Week: Review

Write a brief summary of what Jesus said to you each day this past week and the step of faith he called you to take:

Monday

Tuesday

Wednesday

Thursday

Friday

Saturday

Footsteps Every Week: Reflect

Big Picture
As you look over what Jesus has said to you this past week, do you see any themes? What is the most important thing you need to remember and believe?

Predictable Pattern
As you look over what Jesus called you to do this past week, is there a new predictable pattern he is inviting you to establish in your life with God and others?

Plant the Word
As you look over the readings from this past week, write out the passage that feels most important for you and memorize it over the next week:

DAY 25

READ AND LISTEN: LUKE 6:37-42

Take a minute to listen for what the Spirit is saying in these verses…

COMMENT AND CONSIDER

Jesus began his "Sermon on the Plain" by describing how the values of God's Kingdom are completely backward from what is considered important in the kingdoms of this world. In God's Kingdom you are blessed in the midst of things considered a curse in this world, such as poverty, sorrow, and persecution. On the other hand, the things this world accounts a blessing, like wealth, comfort, and recognition, are the very things that can become curses because they keep us from God's Kingdom. Jesus continued his sermon by calling us to a radical ethic of unconditional, self-giving love. This is at the very heart of what it means to live in God's Kingdom by doing his will on earth as it is done in heaven.

Now we read Jesus' explanation of what *agape* love looks like in our relationships. When we judge people, we withhold the forgiveness that has been so freely given to us. When we condemn people, we withhold the mercy that has been lavished on us. We fail to love others as God has loved us when we live with an attitude of self-righteous superiority, imagining that we are better than those we deem not pious as we are. The problem is that we expect to receive what we are unwilling to give.

Jesus drew on the image of a generous merchant to describe the attitude of those who are living in God's Kingdom. In the kingdoms of this world, people usually give you as little as possible and try to keep as much as possible for themselves. In the ancient world it was common for unscrupulous merchants to use faulty weights or scales to deliver less than you paid for. Jesus described the opposite to illustrate the disposition of those who operate according to the Kingdom of God. In God's Kingdom people operate like a merchant who measures out the grain you have paid for and then presses it down, shaking the container to make room for more grain, which he then fills to overflowing until the excess grain fills the fold at the waistband of your robe!

Jesus said those who are as generous as this merchant, who give as much as possible to others, will receive in kind the same generosity from others and from God. In the kingdoms of this world, the assumption is those who give little will keep much and those who give much will keep little. But in the Kingdom of God, we discover the truth that those who give freely receive freely. Those who use a generous measuring scoop will receive generously from the same scoop.

Jesus warned us not to be influenced by the values of the kingdoms of this world. It does not help you to ask a blind person to guide you if you are blind. You will end up in the same pitfalls as them! We need a guide who can see better than we can to show us the way. If your attitude toward others is shaped by those who operate according to the kingdoms of this world, you will end up in all kinds of trouble.

Actors in the Greek theater used masks to display the various characters in a play, hiding their true selves from the audience. The word for those masks is "hypocrisy," the very word Jesus used to describe those who are being shaped by the values of this world. When we condemn but expect to be forgiven, when we cheat others but expect to be treated fairly, there is an inner contradiction in our very character that amounts to hypocrisy. Jesus gave a comical picture of this hypocrisy when he told of the man walking around with a huge wooden beam sticking out of his eye, pointing out the tiny splinter in someone else's eye!

Are your attitudes and actions toward others being shaped more by the kingdoms of this world or by the Kingdom of God? Who is discipling you? What is the outcome of that discipleship?

Reflect and Respond
What is Jesus saying to me right now?

What step of faith is Jesus calling me to take today?

DAY 26

READ AND LISTEN: LUKE 6:43-49

Take a minute to listen for what the Spirit is saying in these verses…

COMMENT AND CONSIDER

What is the relationship between being and doing? To become effective followers of Jesus, we must be clear on the proper relationship between the nature of our inward self and the nature of our outward actions. The Pharisees believed that doing determined being. If you followed the Law, along with all the myriad interpretations and traditions developed by the rabbis, you could establish your righteous standing as a member of the people of God. Your identity was established by your obedience. Doing determines being.

Jesus offered a very different approach to life. He welcomed people who were not obeying the written Law of the Old Testament or the traditions of the Pharisees. He forgave those who were sinful and did nothing but receive grace and mercy. He told stories of a shepherd who left his 99 sheep in the care of another shepherd to go and search for the one lost sheep. He told of a woman who diligently swept the stone floor of her house in search of a lost coin. He described a Father who shamefully ran through the village to lavish love and acceptance on the son who had publicly shamed him, wished him dead, and then squandered his inheritance on immoral living. Jesus taught and demonstrated radical, even scandalous grace toward those who would receive the new identity he offered as beloved daughters and sons of their Father the King!

Jesus said the result of this new identity is a new way of life. He made it clear that being precedes doing; that doing is meant to be the result of being. Who we are ultimately determines what we do, and not the other way around. One of Jesus' favorite images to describe this critical relationship was fruitfulness. Every person in the ancient world could see which trees produced good fruit and which trees produced fruit that was inedible. *"A good tree doesn't produce bad fruit; on the other hand, a bad tree doesn't produce good fruit."* It is not the fruit that makes the tree good or bad, it is the nature of the tree that determines the nature of the fruit it produces. Being determines doing.

Jesus went on to point out we can determine the identity of the tree by recognizing the kind of fruit it bears. As he said, *"Figs aren't gathered from thornbushes, or grapes picked from a bramble bush."* Only a fig tree can produce figs and only grapevines can produce grapes. It doesn't matter if the thornbush claims to be a fig tree, or the bramble claims to be a grapevine. The question is: what kind of fruit is it producing? The fruit doesn't determine the identity of the tree; it is exactly the opposite. The nature of the tree determines the fruit, but the fruit is how we recognize the identity of the tree. *"For each tree is known by its own fruit."* When acts of generosity and kindness flow from a person's life, you are seeing the nature of their heart. When condemnation and lies flow from a person's life, you are also seeing the nature of their heart.

Jesus directly confronted those who adopted a religious posture in their language and social status but didn't actually follow Jesus' example and teaching. *"Why do you call me 'Lord, Lord,' and don't do the things I say?"* Those who talk about doing God's will but don't do God's will are like builders who don't lay a foundation before building a house. As a professional builder, Jesus knew that only the house built of stones laid directly on the bedrock would stand up to the inevitable storms that will topple a house with no foundation. Those who hear Jesus' voice and then respond by exercising the faith his word produces through concrete actions are building their house on the strong foundation of bedrock. Nothing will shake that house.

That doesn't mean acts of obedience determine standing with God; it means those who have received grace and know they are God's beloved children will listen and obey. That is the good fruit that identifies them as a good tree. Being leads to doing. Doing identifies being. Where do you find your identity? How does that identity shape your actions and your lifestyle? Are you learning to let your being shape your doing?

Reflect and Respond

What is Jesus saying to me right now?

What step of faith is Jesus calling me to take today?

DAY 27

READ AND LISTEN: LUKE 7:1-17

Take a minute to listen for what the Spirit is saying in these verses…

COMMENT AND CONSIDER

The Roman legions were renowned for their organization and discipline, which had allowed them to conquer most of the Mediterranean world by the time of Jesus. Centurions were the backbone of the Roman army, each one commanding about 100 soldiers, called a "century." (For comparison, a legion was made up of 60 centuries or about 6,000 troops.) Thus, a centurion had significant means and position in Roman society and earned about fifteen times as much as a soldier.

Because Capernaum was located on the major trade route called the Via Maris ("Way of the Sea") near the border between Herod Antipas' and Herod Philip's territories, it is not surprising a Roman military camp was nearby to oversee the collection of taxes and control this strategic crossroads. What is surprising is that a Roman officer, no matter how wealthy he might be, would build the local Jewish community a synagogue, especially the one in Capernaum that is the largest from the first century discovered so far in Galilee.

The fact that the leaders of the Jewish community came to Jesus on behalf of this centurion gives us a clue that he was a "God-fearer," a Gentile who had come to believe in and worship the God of Israel. When the elders asked Jesus to heal the centurion's servant, they were saying, *"He is worthy for you to grant this, because he loves our nation and has built us a synagogue."* Roman culture was built on hierarchical relationships of patronage in which more wealthy and powerful "patrons" provided social favors for "clients" who were lower on the socio-economic ladder. Clients, in turn, demonstrated loyalty by serving the patrons and functioning as part of an entourage which elevated their particular patron's social status. The centurion was clearly a patron to the Jewish community, and these elders functioned as his clients by coming to ask Jesus for this healing.

However, as Jesus drew near to the officer's house, the centurion turned the tables by sending friends to tell Jesus, *"Lord, don't trouble yourself, since I am not worthy to have you come under my roof."* Although he was a man of fearsome authority and power, the centurion humbled himself and took the position of a client by asking his patron Jesus to do this favor for him. He also demonstrated sensitivity to Jewish customs because religious Jews considered a Gentile's home religiously unclean.

The centurion was accustomed to one hundred soldiers doing exactly what he told them to do, when he told them to do it, and how he told them to do it. He recognized Jesus carried even greater authority, and that Jesus could simply issue the order from a distance and his servant would be made well. Jesus marveled at this Gentile military officer's confidence in his ability to heal, saying *"I tell you, I have not found so great a faith even in Israel."*

Then, as if healing the servant was not enough, Jesus demonstrated the true scope of his authority when he bumped into a funeral procession for the recently deceased son of a widow. Widows were considered the most vulnerable people in first-century Jewish society, especially if they had lost an only son, because they did not have a male relative to protect and provide for them in a patriarchal culture. Ignoring the religious rules about not touching a corpse, Jesus reached out and touched the funeral bier on which the body was being carried to the cemetery and said, *"Young man, I tell you, get up!"* When the son suddenly sat up, crowds were amazed and praised God for working so powerfully through Jesus.

What authority do you carry? Are you a parent? A boss? A law enforcement officer? An elected official? We all have differing levels of authority in this world based on our title and position. As the centurion understood, Jesus' authority in the Kingdom of God is far greater than the authority granted by any of the kingdoms of this world, which is why God's power flowed through him to do God's will on earth as it is in heaven. As his follower, you have been given the same authority, and the power of the Holy Spirit is present within you if you trust and follow Jesus. How will you exercise the authority given to you so God's power can flow through you more consistently to do God's will?

Reflect and Respond

What is Jesus saying to me right now?

What step of faith is Jesus calling me to take today?

DAY 28

READ AND LISTEN: LUKE 7:18-23

Take a minute to listen for what the Spirit is saying in these verses…

COMMENT AND CONSIDER

After he baptized Jesus, John the Baptist continued his prophetic preaching, delivering a public rebuke of Herod Antipas for having an affair with his half-brother Philip's wife Herodias. Although this rebuke was true, Antipas could not let this direct challenge to his authority go unpunished, so he locked up John in the prison of Machaerus on the east side of the Dead Sea. (See Luke 3:19-20.) We can still visit the excavated ruins of this massive Herodian palace-fortress in Jordan today. As John endured the scorching days and freezing nights in that desert prison, he continued to receive reports of Jesus' unfolding ministry, but they puzzled him. Like most other Jews of the first century, John expected the Messiah to overthrow the Romans in a supernatural show of military force, but Jesus spent time with questionable characters, fed crowds of ordinary people, teaching them to turn the other cheek and go the extra mile.

Certainly, springing John from prison must be part of Jesus' plan of Messianic revolution, John surmised! And yet John sat in that prison, day after day, waiting for deliverance that didn't come. He began to wonder if he had been wrong about his cousin's true identity, and so he sent some of his disciples to ask Jesus directly, *"Are you the one who is to come, or should we expect someone else?"* The subtext of his question was clear: "Why haven't you rescued me from prison and begun your military campaign to overthrow the Romans?"

Luke points out Jesus was busy healing the sick, liberating the spiritually oppressed, and giving sight to the blind when John's disciples arrived. Jesus responded to John's question by reminding them of the same passage from Isaiah 61 he used to launch his public mission in Nazareth: *"The Spirit of the Lord is on me, because he has anointed me to preach good news to the poor. He has sent me to proclaim release to the captives and recovery of sight to the blind, to set free the oppressed, to proclaim the year of the Lord's favor."* (See Luke 4:16-30.) Isaiah prophesied these were the signs the Messiah had come and the Messianic Age was beginning. As Jesus said, *"Go and report to John what you have seen and heard: The blind receive their sight, the lame walk, those with leprosy are cleansed, the deaf hear, the dead are raised, and the poor are told the good news."*

Jesus showed them the kind of Messiah he was. Not a military ruler conquering through violent force, but the Prince of Peace inaugurating the reign of his Father the King in compassion, love, and grace. He demonstrated the Kingdom of God by doing God's will on earth as it is in heaven. Although it was foretold throughout the Prophets of old, this kind of Messiah challenged everyone's expectations. Jesus recognized this when he said, *"Blessed is the one who isn't offended by me."* The religious leaders were threatened by Jesus' authority and power, but they were also offended by the suggestion they could be so wrong about the kind of Messiah God would send to save them. Those who were able to receive and follow Jesus were the ones who were willing to set aside their assumptions and expectations to let Jesus define who the Messiah is and what God's Kingdom is like.

We all carry certain assumptions and expectations of who Jesus should be and what he should do. What are your assumptions about Jesus? What are your expectations of him? How are they different from the real Jesus of the Bible? Are you willing to let go of your presuppositions and submit to the real Jesus by following him?

REFLECT AND RESPOND

What is Jesus saying to me right now?

What step of faith is Jesus calling me to take today?

DAY 29

READ AND LISTEN: LUKE 7:24-35
Take a minute to listen for what the Spirit is saying in these verses…

COMMENT AND CONSIDER

The disciples of John brought their rabbi's question from the Machaerus prison to Jesus: *"Are you the one who is to come, or should we expect someone else?"* (Luke 7:19) Jesus' response was challenging. He did not offer to rescue John but challenged him and all who heard Jesus to accept he was a very different Messiah than they were expecting. Jesus showed them God's Kingdom operates very differently than the kingdoms of this world, and sometimes the imprisoned do not get set free in the time and in the way they want.

After John's disciples left to deliver this message to their rabbi, Jesus praised John in the highest possible terms. He was not a wishy-washy preacher, like a fragile reed, speaking words the people wanted to hear. John was not culturally compromised, swaying in the wind and caught up in the latest trends. Nor was he a well-dressed nobleman, leveraging his position to serve his own comforts and desires. No, he was an ascetic prophet like Elijah who spoke the unvarnished truth he received from God without excuses, even if it landed him in prison.

And yet, Jesus said, John was more than just another prophet; he was the forerunner of the Messiah, fulfilling the prophecies of Exodus 23:20 and Malachi 3:1. He was preparing the way for God's Kingdom to come through Jesus! This is why Jesus said, *"I tell you, among those born of women no one is greater than John, but the least in the kingdom of God is greater than he."* Jesus highlighted the strategic importance of John's role, but he did not create a celebrity culture that valued certain people at a higher level because of the visibility of their service. The anonymous humble servants who get no recognition in this world will be lifted up and celebrated in the Kingdom of God.

Luke tells us the everyday people listening were not offended by the very different Messianic vision Jesus offered them. They had been baptized by

John and trusted Jesus because he was the one John foretold. On the other hand, the religious leaders listening took offense at Jesus, just as they had at John. They had refused John's baptism and now rejected Jesus' message of the Kingdom because it didn't fit their presuppositions. Seeing their stubborn pride, Jesus recalled a common street game called "wedding," in which children danced while someone played an instrument, suddenly stopping when the music stopped. Jesus said of the religious leaders' resistance to his message, *"They are like children sitting in the marketplace and calling to each other: 'We played the flute for you, but you didn't dance; we sang a lament, but you didn't weep!'"*

To demonstrate the false motives of these "children" who refused to dance to Jesus' music, he pointed out that they criticized both Jesus and John for exactly opposite reasons. They accused John of being demonized because of his acetic lifestyle, while alternately condemning Jesus as a glutton for his celebratory parties with morally questionable friends. Damned if you do, damned if you don't! There is simply no reaching people who are not receptive, no matter how the Good News is expressed. Jesus went on to say, *"Yet wisdom is vindicated by all her children."* In the Old Testament "wisdom" was often portrayed as a woman calling people into a life of goodness and godliness. The so-called "sinners" and tax collectors were ready to dance to Jesus' music, and the wisdom of that choice was born out in the good fruit of their changed lives.

Can you hear the music of Jesus' Kingdom? What causes you to resist dancing to the beat of heaven? What would it look like to join in the dance more fully? How can wisdom be vindicated by your life?

Reflect and Respond

What is Jesus saying to me right now?

What step of faith is Jesus calling me to take today?

DAY 30

READ AND LISTEN: LUKE 7:36-50

Take a minute to listen for what the Spirit is saying in these verses…

COMMENT AND CONSIDER

All four Gospels record a woman lavishly anointing Jesus at a banquet in his honor, and Jesus then interpreting her unorthodox actions to those at the table. (See also Matthew 26:6-13, Mark 14:3-9, and John 12:1-8.) In Matthew, Mark, and John, the dinner is set in Bethany shortly before Jesus' crucifixion. It was hosted by Simon the Leper and the woman in Bethany was Mary, the sister of Martha and Lazarus. Jesus interprets this anointing as the woman's prophetic preparation of his body for burial.

By contrast, Luke's account is of an event that happened earlier in the mission of Jesus, before he came to Jerusalem for his final Passover. A Pharisee named Simon had invited Jesus to a banquet at his home. The dinner consisted of the leading men of that town reclining on pillows around the exterior of a low, u-shaped table at which the women were serving the meal. Such meals were public affairs, and even those who were not invited could come listen to the conversation, almost the way we tune into the conversation between celebrities on a talk show.

A Galilean woman labeled by her community as *"a sinner,"* which may mean she was a known prostitute, was also there to watch. Jesus showed a shocking level of forgiveness and acceptance to those the religious leaders had utterly rejected. In fact, Jesus said to the religious leaders, *"Truly I tell you, tax collectors and prostitutes are entering the kingdom of God before you."* (Matthew 21:31) This kind of lavish grace had changed the heart and life of this woman and filled her with unspeakable gratitude.

This brave woman sought to find a way to express her gratitude for the life-changing grace Jesus had shown her. Taking an alabaster bottle of perfume used in her former trade, she entered the dining room and approached Jesus. Although anointing oil was usually applied to the head, she came to his feet first, since he was reclining with his legs extended away from the table. There she knelt.

In Middle Eastern culture, feet are considered the most unclean part of the body. The lowest slave in the household was assigned the unwelcome task of washing feet. Before she could open the bottle of perfume to anoint his head, she began weeping over Jesus' feet and unwound her hair to dry them, enacting her own kind of foot washing. Then, instead of raising herself to Jesus' head, she continued her honorific act of service by kissing his feet and applying the precious oil. That this woman chose to anoint Jesus' feet rather than his head demonstrated the deep humility and inexpressible gratitude with which she came to him.

Meanwhile, the host Simon, oblivious to the powerful act of love and devotion they were all witnessing, could not understand why Jesus was allowing this sinful woman to get close to him. He thought to himself, *"This man, if he were a prophet, would know who and what kind of woman this is who is touching him—she's a sinner!"* Ironically, precisely through his prophetic insight Jesus perceived Simon's judgmental thoughts and so he told him a parable of two debtors, one who owed ten times the amount of the other, and how both debts were forgiven by the creditor.

Jesus asked Simon, *"So, which of them will love him more?"* Simon gave the obvious answer, *"I suppose the one he forgave more."* Jesus went on to point out how little Simon had done to welcome him and how much this woman had done to show him honor. Then he declared, *"I tell you, her many sins have been forgiven; that's why she loved much. But the one who is forgiven little, loves little."*

Are you more like Simon or the woman? Are you stingy with your expressions of love or lavish? Are you aware of how much you have been forgiven? What would it look like to be more lavish in your expression of love for Jesus?

Reflect and Respond

What is Jesus saying to me right now?

What step of faith is Jesus calling me to take today?

Footsteps Every Week: Review

Write a brief summary of what Jesus said to you each day this past week and the step of faith he called you to take:

Monday

Tuesday

Wednesday

Thursday

Friday

Saturday

Footsteps Every Week: Reflect

Big Picture
As you look over what Jesus has said to you this past week, do you see any themes? What is the most important thing you need to remember and believe?

Predictable Pattern
As you look over what Jesus called you to do this past week, is there a new predictable pattern he is inviting you to establish in your life with God and others?

Plant the Word
As you look over the readings from this past week, write out the passage that feels most important for you and memorize it over the next week:

DAY 31

READ AND LISTEN: LUKE 8:1-15
Take a minute to listen for what the Spirit is saying in these verses…

COMMENT AND CONSIDER

Luke describes Jesus' message as "the good news of the kingdom of God." The Kingdom was Jesus' way of describing the way things are when God's will is done here on earth as it is done in heaven. The Kingdom is literally heaven coming to earth! Because God is perfectly good, his will for us is the best possible of all possible realities. That is why his Kingdom is such good news!

One of the characteristics of God's Kingdom is that people are valued, not because of their social status or political title or worldly accomplishments, but simply because they are the beloved children of God. This is why Jesus was so shockingly gracious and welcoming to people who were condemned by the religious leaders or looked down on by society in general.

Women were one of the groups generally devalued in the ancient world. Girls lived under the authority of their father until they were married to their husbands, who then took over control of their lives. Legally, adult women were grouped with children and slaves and had to live under the control of their father or husband, men who had wide latitude to make choices for them and determine their destiny. In the Jewish world, women were not expected to carry out all the requirements of the Law, were not allowed to own property unless their father died with no sons, and were not allowed to divorce their husbands, although husbands could divorce their wives unilaterally. The testimony of a woman was not considered binding in court. Because menstruation conferred ritual impurity, Pharisees generally avoided any contact with women in public outside members of their own extended family. The rabbis thanked God in their daily prayers that he did not make them a woman.

Jesus demonstrated a very different attitude toward women. He publicly affirmed the hemorrhaging woman who surreptitiously touched him, although she was considered ritually impure. He engaged in conversation with the woman at the well, despite her Samaritan origins and morally compromised homelife. As we saw in the previous passage, a notoriously sinful woman was so transformed by Jesus' acceptance and forgiveness that she broke social norms and wept while anointing Jesus' feet. Given Jesus' countercultural posture toward women, it is not surprising that many women were devoted to him and wanted to follow him. What is surprising is that Jesus accepted them as his disciples, because that role was exclusively reserved for men.

Although women in Scripture often remain nameless, reflecting their subordinate position in society, Luke names three specific upper-class women who were so impacted by Jesus' ministry that they not only supported his work financially, but traveled with him and his inner circle of male disciples on missionary journeys. He also says *"many others"* supported Jesus as well. This set the stage for the Apostles who followed Jesus' example by recognizing women as equal partners in marriage, as leaders in the church, and even as fellow apostles. (See 1 Corinthians 7:3-4; 11:5, 11; and Romans 16:1-7.)

Luke sets Jesus' familiar Parable of the Sower and the Seed in the context of these women disciples, perhaps to highlight that they were good soil in which the seed of Jesus' word took root and bore good fruit, multiplying many times over. This parable should probably be referred to as the Parable of the Soils, because that is the point of this powerful little story. The seed falls on hardened soil, shallow soil, and weedy soil, but none of those bear good fruit. The good soil receives the seed, allows roots to go deep, and then sprouts a resilient plant which multiplies the seed in its fruit. Mary Magdalene, Johanna, and Suzanna were certainly good soil that multiplied good fruit!

Are you good soil? How does society's tendency to value some people more than others affect the way you see and interact with those you cross paths with every day? How can Jesus' radical acceptance and affirmation of all people change the way you relate to those who are different than you?

Reflect and Respond

What is Jesus saying to me right now?

What step of faith is Jesus calling me to take today?

DAY 32

READ AND LISTEN: LUKE 8:16-25
Take a minute to listen for what the Spirit is saying in these verses…

COMMENT AND CONSIDER

Jesus knew who he was. He knew who his Father was. He knew the ultimate outcome of history. He knew in the end the incalculable goodness of his Father the King would triumph over injustice, oppression, and evil. Fully participating in that inevitable triumph was the purpose of Jesus' life. This gave Jesus such strength and confidence. This is what it means to seek and live in the Kingdom of God. And this is why he could fall asleep in the midst of a storm that had veteran fishermen crying out in fear for their lives.

Earlier, when the disciples asked Jesus about the parable of the soils, Jesus quoted Isaiah 6:9: *"The secrets of the kingdom of God have been given for you to know, but to the rest it is in parables, so that 'Looking they may not see, and hearing they may not understand.'"* (Luke 8:10) At first this seems a strange statement. Why would Jesus want some people not to see or understand? If we consider the context of Isaiah 6, we realize this verse is simply describing the inevitable judgment coming upon those who persist in unbelief and rebellion against God.

Jesus spoke in parables as a way of sifting out those who were genuinely open and responsive to him ("people of peace") from those who were stubbornly committed to going their own way and becoming a tool of the deceiver. Those who are willing to enter the stories Jesus told and wrestle with what the Spirit was saying through them prove to be God's children and part of his Kingdom. Those who reject Jesus' stories and hold them at arm's length will never understand and follow Jesus.

Each night people in the time of Jesus lit small clay lamps filled with olive oil and set them up high on a special stand or in a small niche built into the wall. As they did, the light spread across the room, and everything in it suddenly came into view. Jesus said that as the Kingdom of God comes into this broken world, everything will be revealed by the light. The enemy tries to block the light so he can carry out his mission to deceive and mislead people away from their true identities as children of God and their destinies to rule on God's behalf. Jesus' teaching and way of life are exactly the opposite, spreading light that reveals the hearts of people for good or for bad. As Jesus said, *"For nothing is concealed that won't be revealed, and nothing hidden that won't be made known and brought to light."*

This is terrifying news for those who are opposed to God, because the true nature of their deeds will become known to everyone. There is no hiding in the light of God's truth. But this is great news for those who are part of God's family and seeking his Kingdom, because the truth about God's goodness and their redemption will also be known to everyone. They discover that when you have been accepted, forgiven, and welcomed into the family of God, there is no need to hide as Adam and Eve did.

Jesus' mother and brothers came to see him at the house of Simon and Andrew in Capernaum, and Jesus' response seems harsh until we realize why they came. They thought Jesus had gone crazy and they were going to take him back home to Nazareth to nurse him back to mental health. (See Mark 3:20-21, 31-35.) Jesus made it clear that the light of the Kingdom reveals our true identity and our true family.

What is the truth about you? Do you know who you are? Do you know why you are here? What parts of your life are being revealed by the light of Jesus' teaching and way of life? What part of you still hides in the shadows, resisting his Kingdom? What does it mean to step more fully into the light of Jesus, so God's Kingdom can come through you more effectively?

REFLECT AND RESPOND

What is Jesus saying to me right now?

What step of faith is Jesus calling me to take today?

DAY 33

READ AND LISTEN: LUKE 8:26-39

Take a minute to listen for what the Spirit is saying in these verses…

COMMENT AND CONSIDER

After calming the storm, Luke tells us Jesus and the disciples sailed *"opposite Galilee,"* which was across from the primarily Jewish, western side of the lake. This eastern side was the region where most of the powerful Greek cities of the Decapolis were located. Luke tells us this deliverance took place in *"the region of the Gerasenes,"* which was one of those Greek cities, but in their textual variants Matthew and Mark locate this event in *"the region of the Gadarenes"* or *"the region of the Gergesenes,"* indicating they knew this demonized man came from the region of the Decapolis, but were unsure exactly which city it was. (Matthew 8:28, Mark 5:1)

Matthew, Mark, and Luke all describe the terrifying storm that nearly sunk their boat immediately before recording this event. It is almost as if Jesus was heading to this Greek area specifically to confront these demons, and the forces of chaos tried to sink his boat before he could even arrive! When he did arrive, a terrifying showdown began to unfold between the kingdom of darkness and the Kingdom of God. Luke tells us this poor man had been horribly dehumanized by the demons that had taken control of him, to the point he was barely recognizable as a man any longer. His animalistic strength was demonstrated by his ability to snap iron shackles and chains. But Jesus was not terrified, in fact he seemed downright calm in the face of this living nightmare. The demons tried to gain the upper hand by using Jesus' name, but he simply responded by demanding theirs instead. When they named themselves *"Legion"* it became apparent this was going to be no ordinary exorcism! A Roman legion typically consisted of about 6,000 soldiers, but this Legion did not put up much of a fight.

Once the demons realized they were up against an infinitely greater power, they switched to negotiating with Jesus for a truce. There is much we don't know about demons, but it seems they don't like to be disembodied. If they gain control of a person, they can do more damage than if they are simply inhabiting the spiritual realm. In this case, they decided that being cast into a herd of pigs was better than being banished to the emptiness of darkness, so they begged Jesus to do this for them. From a Jewish point of view, this was a fitting fate for unclean spirits because pigs, like the tombs where this was all taking place, were considered ritually unclean. Then the ultimate joke was pulled on the legion of demons when Jesus granted their request, but the pigs turned suicidal and drowned themselves in the lake!

The financial loss of such a huge herd of pigs would have caused quite a reaction, but the radical transformation of this formerly demonized man shook the local people the most. He was completely normal again, and this freaked them out. Aware that Jesus possessed a power they had never seen before, but unaware of the source of this power, they were afraid and asked him to leave their region. The transformed man begged Jesus to let him go with him, but instead Jesus said, *"Go back to your home, and tell all that God has done for you."* While the bullseye of Jesus' missional target was the everyday Jews of upper Galilee, he knew this Gentile man would not be an effective missionary in those close-knit communities. By contrast, Jesus knew this man's testimony would be powerful among his fellow Greeks who lived in the cities of the Decapolis. For that reason, Jesus sent this man to be a missionary to his own culture, as the first apostle to the Gentiles!

Some people are called to cross over into a different culture to bring the Good News of the Kingdom to people who are completely different than they are, but most of us are called to be missionaries in the very culture where we are planted. What mission field is Jesus sending you into? What is your testimony of Good News that you can share with people who are open to you?

Reflect and Respond

What is Jesus saying to me right now?

What step of faith is Jesus calling me to take today?

DAY 34

READ AND LISTEN: LUKE 8:40-56
Take a minute to listen for what the Spirit is saying in these verses…

COMMENT AND CONSIDER

When Jesus returned to his hometown of Capernaum, Jairus, a member of the ruling council that organized and oversaw the Sabbath prayer services at the synagogue, approached him. He was one of the leading figures in his community and would have been a widely respected person of means. So, it was shocking when he fell at Jesus' feet in a position of extreme humility. Child mortality was painfully high in the ancient world; about 30% of infants in the Roman Empire died in the first year of their life, and by the age of 15 half had died. A desperate parent is ready to do whatever it takes to save their child. Jairus heard Jesus had the power to heal, so he was willing to publicly shame himself if it would bring his only daughter back to full health. Jesus had compassion on Jairus and immediately went with him to see his daughter.

Meanwhile, an unnamed woman had been in a state of continual menstrual bleeding for twelve years, which rendered her ceremonially unclean. As a result, in addition to dealing with her condition, this woman had spent the last twelve years ostracized from her family and wider community to prevent her from passing on this impurity to others. She had already spent all her money on doctors who were unable to help her. Like Jairus, she was desperate for healing, but unlike Jairus, she was not a highly respected person of means. She was destitute and an outcast in her community, but was a strong and brave woman willing to do whatever it took to get well. Desperate times call for desperate measures.

As Jesus made his way through Capernaum, heading to Jairus' home, a crowd quickly formed and pressed in on him from all sides. This brave hemorrhaging woman saw her opportunity and took it. Pushing her way through the crowd where she was not supposed to be, she approached Jesus from behind and bent down to touch the ceremonial fringe sewn onto the edge of his robe, hoping no one would notice her. However, despite the jostling of the crowd, Jesus was immediately aware that divine power had flowed through him to heal someone, although he did not know who.

Realizing she had been found out, this desperately brave woman came forward, trembling in fear, because she knew condemnation and public scorn would rightly be heaped upon her for knowingly passing on her impure condition to a famous holy man. Like Jairus, she too fell at Jesus' feet, confessing what she had done and why. But instead of denouncing her reckless act, to the surprise of everyone present, Jesus affirmed this woman for her faith and welcomed her into his family when he said, *"Daughter, your faith has saved you. Go in peace."*

In that very moment, a messenger arrived from Jairus' home to report his twelve-year-old daughter had died. Leveraging the powerful faith of the hemorrhaging woman, Jesus told Jairus *"Don't be afraid. Only believe, and she will be saved."* Twelve years of bleeding had just been healed; now twelve years of life was about to be restored! Facing the greatest pain of his life, Jairus clung to Jesus' words and kept putting one foot in front of the other. They arrived at Jairus' home and went in. Once there, Jesus simply said, *"Child, get up!"* and she did!

It didn't matter to Jesus if you were a highly honored man of wealth and power or an outcast woman considered unclean by even her own family. All he cared about was whether you trusted and followed him. Whether you are more like Jairus or this brave woman, Jesus' invitation to you is the same as it was to them: "trust me and follow me." Are you willing to exercise your mustard seed of faith in Jesus today and go where he leads you, no matter how great the fear or how big the challenge?

REFLECT AND RESPOND
What is Jesus saying to me right now?

What step of faith is Jesus calling me to take today?

DAY 35

READ AND LISTEN: LUKE 9:1-17

Take a minute to listen for what the Spirit is saying in these verses…

COMMENT AND CONSIDER

Authority is being put in the position that gives you access to power. In this world people always manage to obtain authority and power whether by sheer determination or dumb luck. Most often they use that authority to serve their own interests. Nearly always they do whatever they can to hold onto power for as long as they can. This is why we often think of authority and power in negative terms. We assume authority will be used to oppress others and power will be wielded to serve yourself.

Herod Antipas was born into a family of worldly authority and power. His father, Herod the Great, passed on to him the authority to rule Galilee and the Roman Senate ratified his choice. Antipas used the power that came from that authority to serve his own desires and build up his own ego. By contrast, Jesus was not born into a position of worldly authority. In fact, the circumstances of his very conception were questionable, and his life as a builder in Nazareth was seemingly very ordinary. But his Father, the King of the Universe, gave him spiritual authority to rule all of creation, confirmed by the heavenly host at his birth! Jesus ultimately used the power that came from that authority to serve others by laying down his life and giving glory to his heavenly Father. Jesus' way of exercising authority and power was so different from Herod's that it filled Antipas with curiosity and fear.

Jesus was revolutionary, not only because of the degree to which he was able to exercise the authority given to him but also because of the selfless way he used the power that flowed from that authority. Even more radical was the way Jesus multiplied his authority in others and gave his power away. Jesus intentionally trained the disciples to do everything they had seen him do, explicitly passing on his authority and power to these men and women. Then he sent them out in pairs on mission to show and tell the Good News of the

Kingdom to people who were receptive. He instructed them not to take the normal supplies you would pack for a journey, but to go in faith and rely on God to provide. And he did provide, more than they could have imagined!

When his disciples returned from doing the things they had learned from their Rabbi, he took them away for a time of rest and debriefing. But the crowds figured out where they were going and met them there. Rather than send them away, Jesus ministered to them and then challenged his disciples to feed the crowd that had grown hungry. When they expressed their inability to do so, Jesus used the opportunity to teach them another lesson in exercising the divine authority and power entrusted to them.

Looking up to his Father in heaven from whom he had received all authority, Jesus offered to him the paltry five loaves and two fish they had managed to scrounge up. Then he passed that authority to the disciples, challenging them to step out in faith by wading into the hungry crowd with what was obviously a ridiculously inadequate amount of food. As a result, the power of God flowed through the disciples to miraculously multiply the bread and fish a thousand times over! The key was they stepped out in faith despite overwhelming feelings of inadequacy. Exercising the authority given to us by Jesus is always an exercise of faith in the face of our weakness. As Jesus said to Paul when he was confronted by his inadequacy, *"My grace is sufficient for you, for my power is perfected in weakness."* (2 Corinthians 12:9)

Do you believe Jesus has transferred his authority to you? Are you willing to exercise that authority by faith, even when confronted by your weakness? Are you ready to lay down your life in order to use spiritual power for others and not for yourself? If so, you will see a dramatic increase of good fruit in your life that lasts.

REFLECT AND RESPOND

What is Jesus saying to me right now?

What step of faith is Jesus calling me to take today?

DAY 36

READ AND LISTEN: LUKE 9:18-27

Take a minute to listen for what the Spirit is saying in these verses...

COMMENT AND CONSIDER

God promised King David, *"I will raise up after you your descendant... and I will establish the throne of his kingdom forever. I will be his father, and he will be my son."* (2 Samuel 7:12-14) In the immediate context, this applied to Solomon, but in the centuries that followed, the Jewish people recognized in these words a deeper promise that a descendant of David would be raised up to save God's people and establish God's rule. The ancient kings of Israel were anointed as a sign of God's authority and blessing. The term *"Messiah"* (Hebrew for "Anointed One") came to designate this royal Savior who was coming to deliver his people.

There were competing views of this anticipated Messiah. Some believed he would be a human king who would defeat Israel's enemies, while others awaited a divine Messiah who would supernaturally destroy all those who opposed God's rule. The community at Qumran prepared for the coming of two Messiahs, a royal and a priestly one. But the common assumption of all these theories was that the Messiah would definitively conquer all Israel's enemies.

The people of Israel had endured centuries of oppression by a succession of pagan invaders, and now the Romans had conquered them. A Roman governor ruled over Jerusalem. The Herodians ruled the rest of the country, serving the purposes of their pagan overlords. Tax collectors extorted everyday people to fill the coffers of Rome and feed Herodian ambitions. Roman soldiers patrolled the streets to enforce their rule. The more the people felt the injustice of this pagan oppression, the more they longed for a Messiah to come and save them from all of it.

So it is no surprise that when Jesus began his public ministry, rumors about him began to fly. Who is this Jesus? When Jesus took his disciples away to Caesarea Philippi in the very north of the country on their final retreat, he asked them about the rumors. After hearing some of the theories people were discussing, Jesus asked the all-important question, *"Who do you say that I am?"* Peter stepped forward in his characteristic way and declared what all the other disciples had been secretly hoping was true, *"God's Messiah."*

Peter was right, of course, but what he meant by "Messiah" was very different from who Jesus was and what his mission was. The disciples assumed that if Jesus was the Messiah, he would lead them to Jerusalem to overthrow Pontius Pilate, kick out the Roman army, and set up a new administration in Herod's massive palace on the western hill of the city. They could just imagine all the luxury, fame, and power that would come from being in Jesus' inner circle. Finally, they would not have to break their backs to support their families and keep the tax collectors at bay! Finally, they would not be humiliated by Roman soldiers forcing them to carry their gear for one mile. Finally, they would be recognized as some of the greatest people in all of Israel and would enjoy the inevitable perks that came from power.

Jesus was fully aware how far off their expectations were, and so he began to explain the true nature of his Messianic mission. He was not going to Jerusalem to establish his earthly rule over Israel, but to lay down his life to establish an eternal Kingdom over all creation for all time. This Kingdom of love and justice would come through suffering and self-sacrifice, and would release the power that overthrows the prince of lies and his kingdom of darkness. If they wanted to be part of his coming Kingdom, they would have to take up their own cross every day and follow in his footsteps.

How do your assumptions about the Christian life align with Jesus' description of the nature of true discipleship? What does it mean for you to take up your cross every day? What is one area where Jesus is calling you to lay down your life?

Reflect and Respond

What is Jesus saying to me right now?

What step of faith is Jesus calling me to take today?

Footsteps Every Week: Review

Write a brief summary of what Jesus said to you each day this past week and the step of faith he called you to take:

Monday

Tuesday

Wednesday

Thursday

Friday

Saturday

Footsteps Every Week: Reflect

Big Picture
As you look over what Jesus has said to you this past week, do you see any themes? What is the most important thing you need to remember and believe?

Predictable Pattern
As you look over what Jesus called you to do this past week, is there a new predictable pattern he is inviting you to establish in your life with God and others?

Plant the Word
As you look over the readings from this past week, write out the passage that feels most important for you and memorize it over the next week:

DAY 37

READ AND LISTEN: LUKE 9:28-36

Take a minute to listen for what the Spirit is saying in these verses…

COMMENT AND CONSIDER

From the very beginning of his public ministry, Jesus attracted people. Something was profoundly different about the way he spoke, the way he lived, the way he interacted with people, and the way he related to God. Not only was Jesus' way of life unique, but his character was also unlike anyone they had ever met. Some people were curious and wanted to see what he would do next. Others were hungry for something deeper and wanted to learn more about him and from him. But some people began to believe what he said was true and decided to pattern their lives after his. Others still were attracted to Jesus but deeply threatened by what he said and did.

Wherever Jesus went he demonstrated God's love, spoke God's truth, and affirmed the value of every person he met. When the crowds of people who wanted to be near him became too big for the synagogues and the towns, he moved into the countryside and sat down on hillsides or in boats near the shore so thousands could hear him teach. He also opened the door of Simon and Andrew's extended family home and welcomed anyone who was interested to come in and spend time with him. Their home, built around a central courtyard, could have held about 50-60 people and was often filled to overflowing. The Gospel writers refer to this group of men and women as Jesus' disciples. Jesus also prayed all night and then intentionally invited twelve men to form his inner circle of disciples and follow him full time. He occasionally took three of those disciples with him for extra investment and training.

These three, Peter, James, and his brother John, went with Jesus up onto a mountain to pray. Matthew and Mark describe it as a *"high mountain"* but don't give us any clues about which mountain it was. (See Matthew 17:1, Mark 9:2.) The highest mountain in the region is Mount Hermon in the very north of Israel, not far from Caesarea Philippi where Peter had just declared Jesus was the Messiah, so it may have been this mountain. Luke tells us they went up to pray. As they prayed something mysterious began happening to Jesus. Matthew and Mark use the word *"transfigured"* to describe this mysterious event. The Greek verb *metamorphoo* means to be visibly changed or transformed. Luke simply describes what happened to Jesus: *"The appearance of his face changed, and his clothes became dazzling white."*

As if this were not dramatic enough, Moses and Elijah appeared with Jesus and talked with him about the tumultuous events coming in Jerusalem that would lead to his *"departure."* Moses represents the Law and Elijah represents the Prophets, signifying that Jesus, the Word of God, is the fulfillment of the entire Old Testament. Both Moses and Elijah had dramatic mountaintop experiences (see Exodus 34:29-35) and the lives of both ended in unique ways; Elijah ascended into heaven as Jesus would, and Moses died alone and was buried by God. (See Deuteronomy 34:1-6 and 2 Kings 2:9-12.) Perhaps they were helping Jesus prepare for the unique end of his life that was coming soon!

How do you respond to such mysterious and amazing events? Peter desperately wanted to hold on to this incredible moment, and so as Moses and Elijah departed, he suggested building three tents, one for each of them to stay in. But moments like these are not meant to be sustained. Instead, the Father spoke a powerful affirmation of Jesus' identity and mission: *"This is my Son, the Chosen One; listen to him!"*

God is bigger than any box we construct for him. Jesus is God. In this moment these three disciples realized there was more to Jesus than they could possibly understand or imagine. What boxes do you construct for God to make him more understandable and manageable? How can you be more open to the inexplicable mysteries of God revealed in Jesus? What will it take for you to have a bigger picture of who Jesus really is?

REFLECT AND RESPOND

What is Jesus saying to me right now?

What step of faith is Jesus calling me to take today?

DAY 38

READ AND LISTEN: LUKE 9:37-50

Take a minute to listen for what the Spirit is saying in these verses…

COMMENT AND CONSIDER

From the time of his earliest memories, Jesus had to deal with people who didn't understand him. His parents had received angelic revelation about his identity which Mary treasured in her heart. Yet when Jesus was 12 and told his parents he must be in his Father's house, they didn't get it. When Jesus announced his Messianic Jubilee in Nazareth, the people of his hometown and even his own family did not embrace the vision. When he told Nicodemus he had to be born again from above, the Pharisee thought Jesus was talking about going back into his mother's womb! Even his closest disciples didn't understand when he was referring to bread as a symbol of spiritual nourishment. It must have been incredibly frustrating for him when people misunderstood his teaching and his mission.

Luke records one of these frustrating moments after Jesus descended from the mountain where he was gloriously transfigured, only to discover the other disciples were not able to deliver a suffering boy. He said rather harshly, *"You unbelieving and perverse generation, how long will I be with you and put up with you?* Then he showed them how to heal this boy. Everyone was amazed, but Jesus reiterated to his disciples what he had told them back in Caesarea Philippi, *"Let these words sink in: The Son of Man is about to be betrayed into the hands of men."* The meaning of Jesus' words could not have been more plain, and yet the disciples did not understand what he was saying. Luke implies a spiritual obstacle blocked their comprehension of these difficult words, but fear is what kept them from asking for clarification. Perhaps they did not want to understand what he was saying.

And then, as if to underscore how completely unaware they were of the true nature of his mission, they began arguing about who was going to have the most powerful position in the cabinet of Jesus' Messianic government. Jesus pointed to the cross, but all they could think about was taking up residence in Herod's palace in Jerusalem. So, Jesus tried a visual aid, calling forward a little child and showing them what greatness looks like in his upside-down Kingdom. He explained that welcoming this child was more important than welcoming kings and emperors. *"For whoever is least among you—this one is great."*

But almost as if they had not even been listening, one of the disciples abruptly told Jesus how they tried to stop someone who was driving out demons in his name. They wanted to protect their special position in Jesus' inner circle and hold on to the spiritual authority he had passed on to them for themselves, when Jesus' words and example clearly demonstrated their calling was to multiply spiritual power by passing that authority on to others. Jesus must have been so weary when he said, *"Don't stop him... because whoever is not against you is for you."*

Why was it so hard for Jesus' closest disciples to understand the true nature of his Kingdom and their calling in it? Certainly, the deceiver was at work blinding their eyes and clouding their minds. Of course, their fallen human nature was hard at work resisting the implications of Jesus' life and teaching despite their best intentions. This is what Jesus meant when he said to them in the Garden of Gethsemane, *"The spirit is willing, but the flesh is weak."* (Matthew 26:41) But it also seems they did not want to hear the hard part of Jesus' message. They filtered Jesus' words and heard what they wanted to hear.

What are your presuppositions about the nature of God's Kingdom? What filters your reading of the Gospels? Is the devil keeping you from seeing the whole picture? Is your self-serving human nature stubbornly resisting the leading of the Spirit? What would it look like for you to take up your cross today and hear the hard words of Jesus that you have failed to understand and embrace in your journey with him so far?

REFLECT AND RESPOND

What is Jesus saying to me right now?

What step of faith is Jesus calling me to take today?

DAY 39

READ AND LISTEN: LUKE 9:51-62
Take a minute to listen for what the Spirit is saying in these verses…

COMMENT AND CONSIDER

Jesus had already told his disciples the destiny that awaited him in Jerusalem. Prophetically he knew he was going to the holy city to be arrested by the religious authorities, beaten, executed, and then rise from the dead. But now the time had come to begin that long, hard road that led to suffering and death. Earlier Jesus said, *"How narrow is the gate and difficult the road that leads to life, and few find it."* (Matthew 7:14) Now the time had come for Jesus to begin the final and most difficult leg of his journey on that road of life. Luke uses a special phrase to describe Jesus' determination to follow that narrow road to the end: "he resolutely fixed his face toward Jerusalem." The ESV translates it *"he set his face to go to Jerusalem."* Eugene Peterson expresses this phrase in the Message as, *"he gathered up his courage and steeled himself for the journey to Jerusalem."*

In moments like these, it is important to remember Jesus' full humanity. It is easy to assume Jesus carried out his mission effortlessly because of his divine nature, but the truth is God emptied himself when he took on flesh and lived truly as a human being on this planet. That means Jesus experienced everything that we do. He faced temptation, he knew pain, he endured fear, and he wrestled with doubt. In this moment he knew where the path of following his Father's will would lead, and he did not want to face it. That was the temptation of Peter's exclamation in Caesarea Philippi, *"Oh no, Lord! This will never happen to you!"* Jesus knew Satan was tempting him to avoid the hard road that lay ahead, which is why he said, *"Get behind me, Satan!"* (Matthew 16:22-23)

In the midst of these very human experiences and spiritual forces, Jesus determined to continue on the path of his Father's will, no matter how steep or treacherous it became. It is fascinating that Luke takes ten more chapters to describe the journey before Jesus made his triumphal entry into Jerusalem. This is a reminder of how much happens along the narrow road! Jesus wasn't just moping along, hanging his head low, and brooding over the hard things that lay ahead. He continued to live with a constant awareness of the Kingdom of God, giving full attention to how the Spirit was leading him to live out his Father's will every day. As Jesus said, *"Truly I tell you, the Son is not able to do anything on his own, but only what he sees the Father doing. For whatever the Father does, the Son likewise does these things."* (John 5:19) Amazing things happen along the narrow road when we determine to follow Jesus no matter what!

This final leg of the journey led Jesus through Samaria, the region Jews normally avoided on their way to Jerusalem. When they were predictably rejected by a Samaritan town, the "Sons of Thunder" said, *"Lord, do you want us to call down fire from heaven to consume them?"* (See Mark 3:17.) Jesus simply rebuked them, and they moved on to another village that received them. Perhaps this was Sychar, the place where John records the amazing encounter with the woman at the well that led to an entire Samaritan village embracing Jesus! (See John 4:4-42.) As they continued along the narrow road, others came and applied to become followers of Jesus. This was the normal way that rabbis chose their disciples, but Jesus often turned it around when he initiated the invitation by saying, *"follow me."* But now he responded to these would-be disciples by warning them of the hard road that lay ahead and explaining that nothing else could come between them and their commitment to him.

Have you set your face toward Jerusalem? Are you aware of the challenges that lie ahead if you continue to follow Jesus? Are you determined to follow his way no matter how hard it gets? Are you ready to put Jesus' will ahead of every other thing that is competing for your allegiance?

Reflect and Respond

What is Jesus saying to me right now?

What step of faith is Jesus calling me to take today?

DAY 40

READ AND LISTEN: LUKE 10:1-16

Take a minute to listen for what the Spirit is saying in these verses...

COMMENT AND CONSIDER

In this passage Luke recounts how Jesus trained his disciples to reach the lost. This is not just a theory, but a detailed description of how Jesus lived out his own mission. When he first met Andrew, Simon, and (probably) John at the Jordan River in the Judean desert where John the Baptist was carrying out his mission, Jesus welcomed these three men to come and spend the afternoon and evening with him. (See John 1:35-42.) He served them a meal, and they spent time getting to know each other. When Jesus left that region and headed north to Galilee, he was rejected by the people of Nazareth, and even his own family did not embrace his vision of the Kingdom, so he went to Capernaum where Andrew, Simon, and John lived. There Simon and Andrew welcomed him into their extended family home and offered hospitality. So, Jesus went with them, stayed with them, ate with them, healed the sick among them, and told them the Good News of the Kingdom. This is exactly the missional methodology that Jesus taught the disciples in this passage!

Just as Jesus had trained and sent out his inner circle of twelve disciples on mission, now he trained and sent the wider circle of disciples who gathered with him in the home of Simon and Andrew in Capernaum. He explained receptive people were out there in need of someone to offer their friendship so they could lead them into the Kingdom of God. He warned them it would not be easy, and they would face opposition, but that they should not arm themselves with worldly resources. Instead, he told them to go in faith so they could learn to rely on God's Spirit to provide what they needed rather than relying on themselves. This is how lambs overcome wolves.

Jesus told them to offer their *"peace"* to people they met, meaning they were to extend their friendship to them. Then he explained, *If a person of peace is there, your peace will rest on him; but if not, it will return to you."* A person of peace is someone who is receptive and responsive to you. They welcome you, listen to you, and serve you. Jesus always offered his peace and observed who would respond to him in kind. To find a person of peace, you first have to be a person of peace yourself. This means a Jesus-shaped missional approach begins by welcoming people, listening to them, and serving them. When they begin to welcome you, listen to you, and serve you, then you know you have found a person of peace.

Jesus explained that once you have found a person of peace, there are five key ways to invest in that friendship. You go with them, entering into their world where they are comfortable. You spend time with them in that setting, getting to know each other and building the friendship. You share meals together because this is a sign of meaningful relationships. Then you raise the spiritual temperature by showing them the power of God's healing love and explaining the Good News of God's Kingdom. But if a person or household or even a whole town are not receptive and responsive to your offer of peace, you move to other places where you can find people of peace, symbolically shaking the dust off your feet to signify that you are not going to get entangled in unfruitful relationships.

This is a simple but challenging approach to relational mission and disciple-making. Are you currently focused on being a person of peace so you can find people of peace? If so, who are the people of peace you are investing in so they can become members of God's family? This is how we live as disciples who make disciples!

REFLECT AND RESPOND
What is Jesus saying to me right now?

What step of faith is Jesus calling me to take today?

DAY 41

READ AND LISTEN: LUKE 10:17-24

Take a minute to listen for what the Spirit is saying in these verses…

COMMENT AND CONSIDER

Jesus told his disciples *"many prophets and kings wanted to see the things you see but didn't see them; to hear the things you hear but didn't hear them."* What made prophets and kings jealous? When he sent out his inner circle of twelve disciples on mission, Jesus gave them *"power and authority over all the demons and to heal diseases."* (Luke 9:1) It is clear he did the same when he sent out the wider circle of 72 disciples on mission, because they returned rejoicing that the power of the Spirit flowed through them to heal the sick and overcome demons. This is what many prophets and kings longed to see and hear but didn't.

Because they don't see the power of the Spirit at work in their midst today, some churches teach or assume the authority Jesus gave his first followers to heal and cast out demons was limited to the Apostles and came to an end when they died. However, here we see the second generation of disciples operating in the same authority and power Jesus gave the twelve disciples. Furthermore, followers of Jesus who were never with him physically during his time on earth, like Paul, also learned to operate in the supernatural power of the Spirit. (See Acts 14:8-10.)

Jesus' authority is available to every follower of Jesus by virtue of their identity as a daughter or son of the King of kings! When we exercise that authority by faith, the power of God flows through us to accomplish his will on earth as it is in heaven. That is how many generations of disciples learned to prophesy, heal the sick, and cast out demons in the power of the Spirit. Even if it is unfamiliar to us or we don't see this kind of power at work in our community of faith today, that doesn't mean it isn't available. It just means we haven't yet learned how to exercise that authority the way Jesus taught his disciples to do it.

As we read the Gospels, we see Jesus didn't heal and cast out demons by asking the Father to do it for him. Instead, he operated as a direct representative of his Father the King by exercising authority over sickness and the devil. Most first-century healers used complex formulas and secret practices in an effort to make people well. Jesus simply commanded sickness to go and declared healing over people. Most first-century exorcists practiced sensational rituals and recited esoteric spells in an effort to deliver people from demonic power. Jesus simply commanded the demons to leave, and they left. This is the difference between trying to overcome obstacles in our own strength and overcoming them by God's power.

When we know our Father is the King of the universe and exercise faith by speaking and acting as his authorized representatives, we become conduits of the Spirit's power to do God's will on earth as it is in heaven. Of course, this does not happen automatically, immediately, or every time. Like every other aspect of the Jesus-shaped life, we grow into these things one step of faith at a time. By following the example Jesus has set for us, studying the Scriptures to grow in our understanding and faith about all of this, and learning from those who are ahead of us on the journey, step by step our spiritual authority will grow. As we choose to exercise that growing authority by faith, we will see the power of the Spirit flowing through us to do God's will more consistently.

As a son or daughter of the King, do you believe God has authorized you to do his will on earth as it is in heaven? Are you seeking to learn how to let the power of the Spirit flow through you more effectively?

REFLECT AND RESPOND

What is Jesus saying to me right now?

What step of faith is Jesus calling me to take today?

DAY 42

READ AND LISTEN: LUKE 10:25-37
Take a minute to listen for what the Spirit is saying in these verses...

COMMENT AND CONSIDER

Jesus' teaching was deeply rooted in the Old Testament, yet it represented a radically new perspective on how to participate in God's plan to redeem all of creation. For instance, when Jesus was asked which is the greatest commandment, he creatively connected a famous passage from Deuteronomy 6:4-5 about loving God, recited every day by devout Jews, and a more obscure passage from Leviticus 19:18 about loving your neighbor as yourself. Jewish teachers were often asked how to attain eternal life. Rabbi Eliezer (AD 90) is reported to have been asked by his pupils, "Rabbi, teach us the ways of life so that by them we may attain to the life of the future world."

When a religious scholar tested Jesus by asking the same question, *"Teacher, what must I do to inherit eternal life?"* Jesus turned the question back on him. This scholar had obviously heard Jesus' teaching about the two greatest commandments, so he quoted Jesus' answer, love God and love your neighbor as yourself. When Jesus affirmed this answer, the man took it a step further asking, *"And who is my neighbor?"* This was a man focused on following the rules, checking the right boxes, and getting the correct answers on the test. He wanted to know the minimum he could do and still get a passing grade. So, Jesus told a story to illustrate the full implications of living in a relationship of love with God that overflows with unconditional love for those around us.

People in Jesus' time were familiar with the well-worn road winding from Jerusalem down through the hills and valleys of the Judean desert to Jericho, which sits nearly 800 feet below sea level in the Jordan Rift Valley. This road was called the Ascent of Adummim, which means "the Red Ascent." This had a double meaning, reflecting the red limestone hills and valleys surrounding the road, but also the blood shed by the many bandits who hid out in the caves of these remote valleys, waiting to attack vulnerable travelers. So it was not surprising to Jesus' listeners that this man was attacked, beaten, and robbed on that route. It was surprising that the two religious leaders chose to ignore this man in desperate need and pass him by.

Levites were the descendants of Levi and took care of the practical needs in the Temple, working as guards, musicians, and janitors. Priests were the descendants of Aaron who carried out the religious functions of the Temple, slaughtering animals, making offerings, and maintaining the incense and showbread in the Sanctuary. Some have tried to excuse them by saying they must have thought the beaten man was dead or pointing out any contact with a corpse would render them unclean and unable to carry out their duties in the Temple. However, Jesus said they were *"going down that road,"* which means they had completed their service in the Temple and were returning home.

A far greater surprise in the story came when Jesus introduced the Samaritan. Ever since the Assyrians invaded the Northern Kingdom of Israel in the eighth century BC and intermarried with the ten tribes, the Jews of the Southern Kingdom had rejected their descendants, the Samaritans, as unclean "half-breeds." This racial prejudice continued until the time of Jesus, and most Jews assumed Samaritans were dishonest and untrustworthy by nature. When this Samaritan went out of his way to care for this Jewish man and spent his own money to ensure he would receive enough care to make a full recovery, it took most of the listeners by surprise, challenging their racist assumptions.

Jesus was powerfully illustrating that our love for God is meant to overflow in radical love and practical service toward every person we encounter, no matter how different they are or what might divide us from them. Who is the least likely person to be considered your neighbor that you will encounter today? What does it look like for you to love that person in concrete, practical terms?

REFLECT AND RESPOND

What is Jesus saying to me right now?

What step of faith is Jesus calling me to take today?

Footsteps Every Week: Review

Write a brief summary of what Jesus said to you each day this past week and the step of faith he called you to take:

Monday

Tuesday

Wednesday

Thursday

Friday

Saturday

Footsteps Every Week: Reflect

Big Picture

As you look over what Jesus has said to you this past week, do you see any themes? What is the most important thing you need to remember and believe?

Predictable Pattern

As you look over what Jesus called you to do this past week, is there a new predictable pattern he is inviting you to establish in your life with God and others?

Plant the Word

As you look over the readings from this past week, write out the passage that feels most important for you and memorize it over the next week:

DAY 43

READ AND LISTEN: LUKE 10:38-42

Take a minute to listen for what the Spirit is saying in these verses…

COMMENT AND CONSIDER

Three siblings, Martha, Mary, and their brother Lazarus, lived in Bethany, a small village that lay just over the Mount of Olives to the east of Jerusalem. Their nuclear families comprised a larger extended family that lived together in an extended family house (Greek: *oikos*). This family and their home in Bethany became Jesus' base of operations in Jerusalem. This encounter in Luke may have been the beginning of their friendship with Jesus, or they may have become friends on one of Jesus' earlier trips to Jerusalem for the great festivals. (See John 2:13; 5:1, etc.)

In any case, Martha invited Jesus into their extended family home, where he began to teach those who gathered in the courtyard and main rooms of the house. In first-century culture, providing generous hospitality was one of the highest expectations, and responsibility for this normally fell to the eldest female of the family. It is clear from Luke's account that Martha was the matriarch who welcomed Jesus and organized the meal for him and his disciples.

In first-century Judaism girls were not allowed to study Torah in the synagogue school taught by the rabbis. Their education was practical training from their mothers and aunts in how to run the extended family home. The boys who studied with the rabbis at the synagogue had the opportunity to apply for advanced studies if they showed enough promise. The best of these students applied to become disciples of the rabbi and were considered the elite leaders of their community.

When Mary chose to sit at Jesus' feet, she intentionally took the posture of a disciple listening to her rabbi. A well-known rabbinical blessing reflected this posture: "Let thy house be a meeting-house for the Sages and sit amid the dust of their feet and drink in their words with thirst." When Paul recounted his pedigree as a disciple of a famous rabbi, he said, *"I am a Jew, born in Tarsus of Cilicia but brought up in this city, educated at the feet of Gamaliel according to the strictness of our ancestral law."* (Acts 22:3) But in the first century, it was completely unheard of and scandalous for a woman to take the position of a disciple!

Martha was scandalized by her younger sister's brazen choice to sit at Jesus' feet and attend to his teaching. It was not only that Mary was failing to help her and the other women with the various tasks required to honor their guests; the bigger issue was the shame she brought on the family by breaking the expectations of traditional gender roles. It is clear Martha had already made every effort to dissuade her sister from her scandalous choice because it was an extraordinary tactic to ask Jesus to intervene in this situation. This was Martha's way of letting Jesus know she was adamantly opposed to Mary's shameful actions.

Martha assumed Jesus would sternly rebuke Mary, which is what any self-respecting rabbi would do when it was brought to his attention that a woman was shirking her responsibilities by sitting at his feet listening to his teaching. But Jesus did exactly the opposite, rebuking Martha, the one who was dutifully doing exactly what society expected of her! He pointed out she was worried and distracted while Mary had chosen the better part by taking the position of a disciple. There is certainly great value in showing honor through hospitality, and there is a time to serve others, but this was not that time. This was a time to sit at Jesus' feet, drink in his words, and learn how to follow him. That was the one thing that was necessary. Martha missed it, and Mary courageously chose it.

What is the one thing that is necessary for you as a disciple today? How can you choose that better part, even if it goes against cultural expectations?

Reflect and Respond

What is Jesus saying to me right now?

What step of faith is Jesus calling me to take today?

DAY 44

READ AND LISTEN: LUKE 11:1-13
Take a minute to listen for what the Spirit is saying in these verses…

COMMENT AND CONSIDER

If we look closely, we have to admit our prayer life is often about us trying to get God to do what we want. Jesus had a completely different orientation. He described it this way: *"Truly I tell you, the Son is not able to do anything on his own, but only what he sees the Father doing. For whatever the Father does, the Son likewise does these things."* (John 5:19) Jesus' prayer life focused on hearing from the Father and aligning himself with his Father's will. His closest disciples recognized something was different about the way Jesus prayed, so they asked him, *"Lord, teach us to pray."*

In response, Jesus taught them this profound model prayer. He did not intend for them to simply memorize and repeat these exact words, although there is certainly value in doing that. Instead, he offered them a framework on which they could build a healthy and fruitful prayer life. A Jesus-shaped prayer life includes worshiping God as King (*"your name be honored as holy"*), seeking God's will above our own (*"Your kingdom come"*), asking for what we truly need (*"Give us each day our daily bread"*), confessing our sins (*"forgive us our sins"*), forgiving others (*"for we ourselves forgive everyone"*), and resisting the temptations of this world and the devil (*"do not bring us into temptation"*).

To put this framework of prayer into context, Jesus told a couple of parables about prayer. The first is based on the strong cultural expectation to provide hospitality for visitors. Someone receives unexpected visitors in the middle of the night but has no bread to offer. So the host goes to their neighbors' house and pounds on the door until he awakens them and convinces them to get out of bed and give him bread to provide hospitality. It would be easy to assume this story is about convincing a stingy God to do what we want him to do, but the message of the parable is that persistence is the key to breakthrough in prayer. This is not because God is stingy and needs to be convinced to give us what is good, but because there are so many obstacles preventing God's will from being done.

To make this clear, Jesus told another parable about prayer, illustrating that a good father would never give bad things to his children. God is good and wants to give us what is good. He is not stingy! We don't need to convince him! We need to keep asking because we live in a broken world where things constantly happen that are not God's will. We need to keep seeking because our flesh naturally resists God's will and needs to learn how to submit to the Spirit. We need to keep knocking on the door of God's will because an enemy of our soul is actively working to thwart God's will, and he needs to be defeated.

Prayer is not about changing God; it is about changing us. It is not about convincing God to do what we want; it is about bringing our heart and mind into alignment with God's will so we can overcome the obstacles to his will. When we recognize God is the King and we actively pray for his rule rather than our own, we begin to hear his voice and see what he is doing. Then we will know what is good and right. Then we will know what we should be seeking after in prayer. If we ask for a snake or a scorpion, our good Father is not going to give it to us. But if we learn what is truly good and persistently ask for bread, eggs, and fish, then our prayers will align us with the will of God, and the Holy Spirit can begin to work through us to overcome opposition and accomplish God's will on earth as it is in heaven.

What are you seeking in your prayer life? How can your times of prayer bring you into closer alignment with God's will?

Reflect and Respond

What is Jesus saying to me right now?

What step of faith is Jesus calling me to take today?

DAY 45

READ AND LISTEN: LUKE 11:14-26

Take a minute to listen for what the Spirit is saying in these verses...

COMMENT AND CONSIDER

Jesus' opponents could not refute the fact that he miraculously healed the sick and supernaturally cast out demons, because the testimonies of these acts were so many and so credible. All they could do was to cast aspersions on the source of Jesus' power by suggesting he was in league with the devil and using demonic power to accomplish his miracles. Jesus responded by pointing out the logical absurdity of such a notion. How can evil power overcome an evil power? As Jesus said, *"Every kingdom divided against itself is headed for destruction, and a house divided against itself falls."*

His Jewish hearers would have immediately thought of the civil war that divided the people of God into the northern kingdom of Israel from the southern kingdom of Judah in the tenth century BC. This rift within the people of God led to their defeat by successive waves of pagan invaders, the most recent of which was the subjugation of the divided Hasmonean dynasty by the Roman army. Satan would never use his power to undermine the influence of his own demons. Furthermore, Jesus went on to point out that other Jewish exorcists claimed to deliver people from evil spirits, but no one accused them of being in league with the devil.

Instead, Jesus pointed out the only reasonable explanation for his ability to drive out demons was that he operated in the authority of his Father the King, and it was God's infinitely greater power flowing through him that overcame demons! He said, *"If I drive out demons by the finger of God, then the kingdom of God has come upon you."* The repeated demonstrations of Jesus' authority and power was affirmation that God was bringing his reign to earth through Jesus. Centuries earlier Isaiah had prophesied these very things would happen when the Messiah came: *"Then the eyes of the blind will be opened, and the ears of the deaf unstopped. Then the lame will leap like a deer, and the tongue of the mute will sing for joy..."* (Isaiah 35:5-6)

Jesus told a short parable to prove his point. If a warlord has a secure castle and is armed with superior weapons, he can guard his possessions from bandits who attack. But if a stronger warlord comes along, he can break into that castle, tie up the first warlord and steal his valuables. The devil was that strong man secure in his castle until Jesus came along, tied him up with the greater authority he received from the Father, and released the plunder of people under the devil's influence and control. Jesus illustrated the irrefutable fact that he repeatedly delivered people from the dehumanizing power of evil by the power of God.

Although the devil is far more powerful than we are, the Good News is a strong man has come to subdue Satan, tie him up, and set us free from his influence and control. But it is not enough to be delivered from the power of evil, because that just creates a vacuum inside of us that can be filled with the power of even more evil spirits. Once Jesus delivers us from the power of the enemy, we need to be filled with the power of the Spirit to live the fruitful life meant for us.

How do you deal with the influence of evil in your life? The devil is *"prowling around like a roaring lion, looking for anyone he can devour."* (1 Peter 5:8) He is that thief Jesus warned about who constantly seeks *"to steal and kill and destroy"* the flock of God. By contrast Jesus said, *"I have come so that they may have life and have it in abundance."* (John 10:10) The question is, under which power will we live: the power of evil that seeks to destroy us or the power of Jesus who leads us into a more abundant life?

All those who say yes to Jesus and submit to him are set free from the power of evil and filled with his far more powerful Spirit. In what area of your life do you need to be set free from the power of the evil one? How can you submit to Jesus and be filled with his Spirit in that area today?

REFLECT AND RESPOND

What is Jesus saying to me right now?

What step of faith is Jesus calling me to take today?

DAY 46

READ AND LISTEN: LUKE 11:27-36

Take a minute to listen for what the Spirit is saying in these verses…

COMMENT AND CONSIDER

Being a celebrity is different than being famous. A person gains fame by doing something extraordinary. A celebrity is known for being well-known. The focus of celebrities is themselves. They spend a huge amount of time and energy curating their public personas and cultivating their fan bases. People who are simply famous are not focused on their fame; they are focused on the things that made them famous—their passion, their art, their sport, their vocation, their cause, their achievement. Jesus was famous, but he rejected celebrity status. Even though he is the only person who ever walked the earth who is worthy of our worship, he did not make himself the focus. He made his Father and his Father's Kingdom the focus of his mission. He was not looking for fans; he was looking for followers.

A woman in the crowd who was listening to Jesus shouted out, *"Blessed is the womb that bore you and the one who nursed you!"* In the honor/shame culture of the ancient world, it was common to compliment someone by congratulating their mother. Objectively this statement was undeniably true. How blessed Mary was to be the means by which God took on human flesh and entered into this world! And yet Jesus, without denying her compliment, redirected the focus away from himself and onto his message of hearing and doing the will of God. This is an example for all those who gain the public spotlight. Remember it is not about you; it is about the mission, the message, the purpose to which you have been called.

As the numbers of those who were drawn to Jesus continued to increase, he became increasingly skeptical of their motives. People in the crowd demanded that Jesus perform impressive miracles. (See Luke 11:16.) They tried to make Jesus into a celebrity who would build his fan base by giving them what they wanted. Instead, Jesus gave them a stern rebuke. *"This generation is an evil generation. It demands a sign, but no sign will be given to it except the sign of Jonah."* Jesus chose to stay focused on his mission and his message rather than give in to the allure and pressure of celebrity status.

Jonah was a prophet of Israel famous for his resistance to call the pagan people of Nineveh to repentance. When God used a huge fish to keep Jonah on the path of his calling, he did preach to the Ninevites, and amazingly they repented! But Jonah was disappointed because he wanted these pagans to be condemned. Ever since the people of Nazareth tried to kill Jesus when he declared the Kingdom of God was for Gentiles too, it had been clear that Jonah's lack of grace towards the Ninevites lived on in many of the Jewish people of Jesus' time. The *"sign of Jonah"* was a reminder to these people that God refuses to give up on anyone and is calling all people, regardless of their heritage or failures, back to himself. It was also a prophecy that, just as Jonah had spent three days in the belly of a fish, so Jesus would spend three days in the darkness of death before emerging to declare God's victory over sin and death! (See Matthew 12:40.)

Jesus' rejection of celebrity status and his challenging words to the consumeristic crowds drove his fans away but rooted his disciples in the mission and the message. (See John 6:60-69.) Rather than seek celebrity status and the self-serving perks it provides, Jesus' disciples learned to lay down their lives in love for others, and the result was a movement of God that is still changing the world 2,000 years later! Disciples of Jesus never seek celebrity status even if they happen to become famous. What are you seeking? Where is your focus? Are you looking for approval from others? Do you crave credit for the things you have done? Or are you focused on the mission and the message of the Good News of the Kingdom?

REFLECT AND RESPOND

What is Jesus saying to me right now?

What step of faith is Jesus calling me to take today?

DAY 47

READ AND LISTEN: LUKE 11:37-54

Take a minute to listen for what the Spirit is saying in these verses...

COMMENT AND CONSIDER

The scribes and rabbis of Jesus' time had tremendous social and religious power among the Jewish people. They were experts in the Law of the Old Testament and memorized the interpretations of generations of rabbis who had gone before them, what is called the "Oral Law." The Pharisees were considered elite among religious leaders because of their zealous commitment to follow even the most obscure or miniscule details of these religious rituals that were added to the Word of God.

There was tremendous pressure on Jesus to align himself with the recognized religious teachers, in particular the powerful Pharisees, because they held great sway with the people and could profoundly influence public opinion about him. But Jesus refused to compromise the truth of God's Kingdom to gain approval from the Pharisees. In fact, he seemed to go out of his way to criticize them, even if it meant major confrontation. This indicates how far off the legalistic, hyper-religious culture of these teachers was from Jesus' vision of the Kingdom.

Because Jesus had become so popular and famous, many religious leaders wanted to share in the recognition he received by hosting lavish banquets in his honor. Jesus accepted these invitations, even if he knew the motivation was flawed. This reminds us that Jesus accepted and welcomed anyone who was willing to repent and follow him, whether they were a religious dignitary or religious outcast. But this doesn't mean Jesus submitted to the legalistic rituals of his hyper-religious hosts. On the contrary, he seemed to intentionally reject the traditions he felt were contrary to the Kingdom of God.

In this case, Jesus accepted a Pharisee's invitation to a banquet, but when he entered the home, Jesus did not follow the intricate rules of ritual hand washing the Pharisees taught. When his host took obvious offense, Jesus began a highly challenging critique of the Pharisees' hypercritical religious culture. He compared them to a stone cup which could be ritually cleansed, unlike pottery dishes which had to be thrown away when touched by someone or something considered ritually impure. But Jesus described them as if they were only cleansing the outside of the cup, meaning the inside would continue to convey impurity. In the same way, the Pharisees were so obsessed with their external religious rituals they ignored the state of a person's heart and mind, or the importance of concrete acts of love and justice.

Then Jesus began to pronounce a series of woes, warning them of the judgment to which they were liable. He warned the Pharisees about their over-emphasis on trivial symbolic practices, like tithing ten percent of their tiny herb gardens while ignoring God's call to love God and neighbor. He warned them about seeking human recognition and approval instead of seeking to live according to the principles and practices God approves. He even accused them of corrupting unsuspecting people by these false teachings, like someone who accidentally walked over an unmarked grave and became ritually defiled without realizing it.

Jesus' indictment of the Pharisees was so harsh, another religious leader who was not a Pharisee appealed to Jesus, asking him to moderate his criticism. Instead, Jesus turned his critique to the wider group of scribes and rabbis and applied the same standard of integrity to them. He confronted them about not practicing what they preach. From the murder of righteous Abel in the first book of the Bible (see Genesis 4:8) to the murder of the prophetic priest Zechariah in what was the last book of the Hebrew Bible (see 2 Chronicles 24:20–22), Jesus illustrated the glaring hypocrisy of honoring certain individuals in public while criticizing them in private.

What hypocrisy in your life needs to be confronted? Who are the people you are called to confront, even if it makes people feel uncomfortable? How can you speak that truth in love without watering down the importance of the message God has given you to deliver?

Reflect and Respond

What is Jesus saying to me right now?

What step of faith is Jesus calling me to take today?

DAY 48

READ AND LISTEN: LUKE 12:1-12
Take a minute to listen for what the Spirit is saying in these verses…

COMMENT AND CONSIDER

Fear is a powerful motivator. We are often unaware of the many ways we are driven by controlling fears. We are afraid of what others might think or say about us. We are afraid of losing what we have. We are afraid of not getting what we need. We are afraid of being hurt by people close to us. We are afraid of being abandoned and alone. We are afraid of being trapped and powerless. The list goes on and on. Controlling fears are different than healthy respect for things that can destroy us. Controlling fears come from a lack of faith in the love of a good God. Healthy respect for spiritual danger comes from submitting to the wisdom and will of God.

Jesus lived a life free from controlling fears because he knew who he was and who his Father was. As John told us, when we live surrendered to the God who loves us perfectly, there is no room for controlling fears in our lives. (See 1 John 4:18.) But Jesus points out we need healthy respect for the things that can derail or hinder our walk with him. One of those is religious hypocrisy. Like yeast spreading silently and unseen throughout a lump of dough, the inconsistency between the interior life of the Pharisees and their external façade of religiosity can creep into our lives as we seek to live according to God's will. Just as Jews sweep their houses clean of yeast every year at Passover, Jesus said we should diligently sweep this insidious inconsistency out of our lives and learn to be on the outside what we are on the inside.

We often hide things from others because we are afraid they will discover our shame or our self-serving motives. But Jesus shows us hiding is futile, because in the end the things we think we have hidden from others will be revealed to all. The secrets we have whispered in the darkness will eventually be shouted from the rooftops. So it is better to bring these things into the light now where we can deal with them. The healthy fear that should motivate us is not what can happen to us in the physical world here and now, but the spiritual damage religious hypocrisy can cause to our souls for all eternity.

Trying to hide our faults and failures from God is the ultimate exercise in futility. He already knows everything about us! God knows the number of hairs on our head. As the writer of Proverbs says, *"The eyes of the Lord are everywhere, keeping watch on the wicked and the good."* (Proverbs 15:3) We are far more precious to him than the sparrows he constantly watches over, even though they were sold for pennies in the marketplace. We don't have to be afraid of being completely open and honest with our loving heavenly Father because his love sets us free from controlling fears.

Because we know God is our loving Father who will never leave us or forsake us, we don't have to be afraid of what might happen to us in this world. Jesus had set his face toward Jerusalem, and he prophetically knew the fate that awaited him there was the fate many of his followers would ultimately face as well. But even if we are called to make the greatest sacrifice in this world, we don't have to be afraid because we know God is the great Redeemer who will turn even the greatest suffering and injustice into something truly good. Jesus promised the Holy Spirit will be with us, giving us exactly what we need to trust him and do his will, even in those most difficult moments! In the end, the only thing for us to fear is our rejection of Jesus by willfully resisting the work of the Holy Spirit who is planting faith in our hearts.

What are you afraid of? How can you let the perfect love of God cast out those controlling fears? For what do you need more healthy respect?

Reflect and Respond

What is Jesus saying to me right now?

What step of faith is Jesus calling me to take today?

FOOTSTEPS EVERY WEEK: REVIEW

Write a brief summary of what Jesus said to you each day this past week and the step of faith he called you to take:

MONDAY

TUESDAY

WEDNESDAY

THURSDAY

FRIDAY

SATURDAY

Footsteps Every Week: Reflect

Big Picture
As you look over what Jesus has said to you this past week, do you see any themes? What is the most important thing you need to remember and believe?

Predictable Pattern
As you look over what Jesus called you to do this past week, is there a new predictable pattern he is inviting you to establish in your life with God and others?

Plant the Word
As you look over the readings from this past week, write out the passage that feels most important for you and memorize it over the next week:

DAY 49

READ AND LISTEN: LUKE 12:13-21
Take a minute to listen for what the Spirit is saying in these verses…

COMMENT AND CONSIDER

Inheritance laws were specified in Numbers 27:1-11 and Deuteronomy 21:15-17 and expanded upon by the rabbis. One of the principles of inheritance was that the eldest son received a double portion, or twice as much as the other sons. This is the "birthright" that Jacob tricked his older brother Esau into giving to him for a bowl of stew. (See Genesis 25:29-34.) Daughters did not receive an inheritance unless there were no sons. One day a man approached Jesus about a dispute he was having with his brother regarding their family inheritance, probably over the correct proportion of the inheritance each should receive.

Rabbis were often asked to rule on these kinds of disputes because of their expertise, not only in the written Law of the Old Testament but also in the memorized teachings of the Oral Law. It is interesting that, although Jesus accepted the title "Rabbi," he explicitly refused to take on this role of arbitrator, at least in this case. Perhaps it was because the man didn't ask Jesus to mediate between him and his brother, but rather instructed him to rule in his favor! Jesus could see this man valued possessions over relationships, and he used it as an opportunity to address the deeply rooted human tendency toward greed.

In the agrarian society of the ancient world, fertile land equaled wealth because the more land you had, the more crops you could plant, and the larger your harvest would be. In this parable Jesus described a man who owned a large tract of land and thus was rich. He was able to harvest more crops than he needed to provide for his needs and wants, so he began to accumulate excess grain and goods. Archaeologists regularly discover stone-lined pits dug in the ground which served as silos to store grain. If kept dry, seeds could last almost indefinitely in such a silo. Some seeds from the first century have even been planted in modern times and sprouted to revive ancient strains of wheat and barley!

This man had such a large surplus from his harvests that his silos were full, even after selling as much of the crop as he could, so he had the dilemma of what to do with all that excess. Rather than selling it at a cheaper price or giving it to the poor, he decided to build bigger barns with more silos so he could hoard his crop and sell it when the price was higher. The point of storing up his crop was to give this man a sense of security and peace. As he said to himself, *"You have many goods stored up for many years. Take it easy; eat, drink, and enjoy yourself."* But he miscalculated where true fulfillment and security come from. When death unexpectedly showed up at his doorstep, God declared him a *"fool."* The Greek word here is *aphron,* which describes someone who is not only stupid, but also morally and spiritually flawed. (See Psalm 14:1.)

Jesus was not against enjoying and multiplying the good things of creation. In fact, he was often criticized for eating and drinking at banquets with generous amounts of food and wine. Jesus often spoke about money and how to use material goods, but his message was always about wisely investing our possessions so they will bless others and extend the Kingdom of God. The problem comes when we hoard our possessions and start to find our security and fulfillment in the accumulation of wealth. There is a strong allure to acquire money, and once you have it, there is often an addictive desire for more. Jesus warns us that this kind of greed is a trap which will keep us from living the truly abundant life he came to give us.

What are you doing with the possessions and resources you have been able to accumulate? Are you finding ways to hold on to them, or are you investing them in a way that will bless others and extend God's Kingdom? Where are you finding your security and sense of fulfillment? Is it in the possessions you have or in the One who gave them to you?

REFLECT AND RESPOND

What is Jesus saying to me right now?

What step of faith is Jesus calling me to take today?

DAY 50

READ AND LISTEN: LUKE 12:22-34
Take a minute to listen for what the Spirit is saying in these verses…

COMMENT AND CONSIDER

What are you seeking? What is most important to you? What outcomes do you hope for? In my culture we are told if you study hard and get good grades, you will get into a good university. If you study hard there and get a good degree, you will get a good job. If you work hard at that job, you will be able to buy a big house, drive a nice car, take fancy vacations, and then you will be fulfilled. Most cultures have a version of this fantasy, but they are all lies. There is nothing wrong with studying and working hard, but achieving these things will not ultimately fulfill you. True and lasting fulfillment flows from being in a loving relationship with God and those around us and living in a way that is true to those relationships. Any other good thing that comes to us beyond this is made worthwhile in the context of these faithful relationships.

Jesus described the reality that comes from living rightly in right relationships as "the Kingdom of God." This reality is what happens when God's will is done on earth the way it is constantly and perfectly being done in heaven. The reason heaven is such a good place is because the God who is perfectly good rules perfectly there. The Kingdom of God comes when that heavenly reality, the reign of God, breaks into this broken, imperfect reality we call earth.

Jesus addressed the anxiety and fear we experience when God's will is not done on earth by promising that God's Kingdom is coming and that we get to be part of it. In the Garden of Eden, when Adam and Eve chose to go their own way, they lost their identity as bearers of God's image and forfeited the dominion they were given to rule creation on behalf of their Father the King. Jesus came to restore our identity as the daughters and sons of our heavenly Father, and he reinstated our birthright to be co-regents with the

King of Creation for all of eternity. This is what Jesus meant when he said, *"Don't be afraid, little flock, because your Father delights to give you the kingdom."* This might be the greatest promise in all of Scripture, because if we have the Kingdom of God, we have everything that matters!

Jews in first-century Palestine lived under the double-burden of taxation by the Romans and the Herodians, and many people lived at the subsistence level, trying to make it from day to day. The anxiety of putting food on the table and clothes on your back were very real pressures. Even so, Jesus explained life is about so much more than seeking these basic necessities. Using the natural environment around him as a compelling visual aid, he pointed out how well God feeds the ravens, who were considered worthless by Jews because they were labeled unclean animals. He noted that the blooming wildflowers, so plentiful on the hills around the Sea of Galilee, were clothed in purple robes as lovely as King Solomon's. He highlighted the futility of worrying about the length of our lives when we have no power over this. If God cares for birds and flowers, which are relatively inconsequential, how much more will he care for you and me, his beloved children? This is why we don't have to live in anxiety or fear, because our Father is the King, and his Kingdom is ours!

This is why Jesus tells us the Kingdom is to be our highest priority and the central focus of our life. Every other good thing will come to us as a result of faithfully living in right relationships with God and those around us. What are the top priorities of your life? What are you focused on? How does Jesus' promise of the Kingdom change that? What does it mean to seek his Kingdom first?

Reflect and Respond

What is Jesus saying to me right now?

What step of faith is Jesus calling me to take today?

DAY 51

READ AND LISTEN: LUKE 12:35-48
Take a minute to listen for what the Spirit is saying in these verses…

COMMENT AND CONSIDER
In biblical times people lived in extended family homes where multiple nuclear families lived and shared life together in common meals and a family business. These extended families (Greek: *oikoi*) included blood relatives, close friends, employees, servants, and slaves. A wealthy *oikos* could have many slaves with various responsibilities helping run the household and the family business. The senior slave or servant was usually called the *oikonomos* (literally "the ruler of the extended family") and had responsibility for all the other slaves, management of the household, and the functioning of the family business. In a wealthy *oikos*, this was a powerful position that wielded great authority for decision-making.

After addressing unhealthy attachment to worldly possessions, Jesus offered an analogy from the extended family system to illustrate how his followers are to use their gifts and manage their resources until the Son of Man returns in glory to set all things right. He described servants who are responsible for the home while the master and the rest of the family are away at a wedding celebration. In the ancient Middle East, weddings often lasted a week or more, and schedules were much less precise than in the modern world, so there was not a set day and time that the family was due to return. This meant the servants didn't know exactly when their master was going to walk through the front door.

If the master returned unexpectedly, irresponsible servants would be caught abusing the master's trust and failing to fulfill their obligations. But servants who diligently fulfilled their responsibilities without the oversight of their master proved to be trustworthy and faithful. Jesus exhorted his listeners to be like these faithful servants, with lamps lit and ready to serve by *"girding their loins,"* which means tying the loose ends of your robe around your waist so you can move freely to serve others. Shockingly, Jesus said the master would gird *his* loins and invite these faithful servants to recline at *his* table while *he* served *them*! This is reminiscent of the messianic prophecy, *"On this mountain, the Lord of Armies will prepare for all the peoples a feast…"* (Isaiah 25:6)

Jesus compares his return to the surprise attack of a thief digging through the mudbrick wall of a locked house to rob a family. The point is that Jesus' return will be unexpected, and so we need to live in constant readiness by faithfully doing the will of God regardless of when he will return. Jesus continued the analogy by saying that those servants who proved to be faithful would be promoted to the position of household manager (Greek: *oikonomos*) and given increased authority and power to manage the extended family home and business. But even greater accountability will apply to the servant in this position of greater authority. If they knowingly take advantage of their master's absence and abuse the master's trust, they will suffer even greater punishment. But the servant who fails to do their job because they are unaware of all their responsibilities will not be judged as harshly. Jesus sums up his point by saying, *"From everyone who has been given much, much will be required; and from the one who has been entrusted with much, even more will be expected."*

It is easy to forget we live in the time between Jesus' first and second coming. We are those servants in charge of the household while the master is away, and we don't know when he will return. The question is, how will we use the freedom and responsibility we have been given? Will we abuse the master's trust and use our freedom to serve ourselves, or will we faithfully fulfill the calling we have been given to be good stewards of our master's resources? If we are good stewards, we will be given more authority and more responsibility, but we will also be held to an even higher standard of accountability. What are you doing while your master is away?

REFLECT AND RESPOND

What is Jesus saying to me right now?

What step of faith is Jesus calling me to take today?

DAY 52

READ AND LISTEN: LUKE 12:49-59

Take a minute to listen for what the Spirit is saying in these verses...

COMMENT AND CONSIDER

Because Jesus' message and demonstration of the Kingdom centered on the grace and love of God for all people, it is easy to assume the way of Jesus automatically leads to peace and reconciliation with everyone around us. However, Jesus' message came into direct conflict with the self-serving nature of fallen humanity and the powers of darkness that conspire to steal, kill, and destroy what is good in this life. This means the way of Jesus' Kingdom inevitably leads to confrontation with the kingdoms of this world and the kingdom of darkness. We see this most clearly in the religious leaders who were so threatened by Jesus' authority they began conspiring to put him to death.

However, Jesus foretold the conflict between light and darkness would find its way into even our closest relationships. Jesus himself experienced this when his own family didn't embrace his vision of the Kingdom of God, failed to stand with him when the people of Nazareth turned violent toward him, and finally decided he had lost his mind. (See Luke 4:28-29; Mark 3:21.) Jesus said the same kinds of division will come into the families of those who decide to follow him and seek his Kingdom. Even though Jesus promised his disciples a transcendent peace (See John 14:27.), he warns us the source of this peace will spark a kind of civil war that pits *"father against son, son against father, mother against daughter, daughter against mother, mother-in-law against her daughter-in-law, and daughter-in-law against mother-in-law."* (See Micah 7:6.)

Jesus expressed the inevitability of this conflict when he said, *"I came to bring fire on the earth, and how I wish it were already set ablaze!"* John the Baptist foretold this when he said of Jesus, *"He will baptize you with the Holy Spirit and fire. His winnowing shovel is in his hand to clear his threshing floor and gather the wheat into his barn, but the chaff he will burn with fire that never goes out."* (Luke 3:16-17) Jesus came with a message of peace and reconciliation, but he knew that the redemption of creation would have to come through a global crisis dividing those who refuse to submit to God's good and perfect will from those who are wholly given over to his rule and reign.

This conflict between light and darkness is nothing new, but the way Jesus chose to fight and win the battle was completely unprecedented. He set his face toward Jerusalem, and as Jesus drew nearer and nearer to the Holy City, he became increasingly aware of the fate that awaited him there. His followers sensed a conflict was coming in Jerusalem, but they assumed Jesus would seize control of the government, take up residence in Herod's palace, and lead an army to overthrow the Roman occupiers. How wrong they were! In anguish Jesus said, *"I have a baptism to undergo, and how it consumes me until it is finished!"* The fiery baptism Jesus was about to experience was rejection, condemnation, torture, and execution, and he knew this was the only way to overcome the power of darkness. Jesus chose to fight this inevitable battle by laying down his life and so to overcome evil with good.

He told his disciples they needed to learn how to interpret the spiritual seasons just as they had learned to interpret the signs of the natural seasons in the sky. A storm is coming, and we had better be ready! Switching to a legal analogy, he told them if they were aware of what was coming, they would be sure to settle their accounts with God before arriving at the place of final judgment.

Do you naively assume following Jesus will bring peace with everyone, or are you prepared for the inevitable battles that will come, even with those who are closest to you? Are you willing to follow Jesus' example of fighting those battles by laying down your life for others? Are you ready for the inevitable global crisis that is sure to come?

Reflect and Respond
What is Jesus saying to me right now?

What step of faith is Jesus calling me to take today?

DAY 53

READ AND LISTEN: LUKE 13:1-17

Take a minute to listen for what the Spirit is saying in these verses…

COMMENT AND CONSIDER

When the newly appointed Roman governor of Judea, Pontius Pilate, displayed pagan symbols in Jerusalem in AD 26, thousands of Jews gathered outside his palace in Caesarea on the coast of Israel in a powerful protest. When Pilate threatened to have his soldiers kill them, they all knelt down and bared their necks, declaring they were prepared to die to defend the sanctity of the Temple. Pilate was forced to back down and remove the pagan standards. Another time Pilate took money from the Temple treasury to pay for the construction of an aqueduct in Jerusalem, and riots broke out. This time he surrounded the protesters with Roman soldiers and began killing the protestors until the crowds dispersed.

Jesus referred to a similar incident of brutality when Pontius Pilate killed Galilean pilgrims who brought sacrifices to the Temple. We don't have other records of this massacre, but it certainly fits with what we know about this ruthless governor. Jesus' point was that the Galileans who suffered such a terrible fate were not punished because they were worse sinners than anyone else. The truth is we are all sinners in need of repentance. Likewise, Jesus referred to the collapse of a tower near the Pool of Siloam in the southeastern corner of the walled city of Jerusalem that killed eighteen people. This was not some kind of special punishment from God. We all need to repent if we are to ultimately avoid the same fate.

Often we assume *"repentance"* is simply feeling bad about our sins, but the Greek word here is *metanoia*, which literally means "to have a change of mind." Biblical repentance is listening for God's voice and allowing him to change our perspective. Those who repent start to see things the way God does and respond in faith. As Paul said, *"So faith comes from what is heard, and what is heard comes through the message about Christ."* (Romans 10:17) Repentance plants faith in our hearts. Exercising that faith one step at a time is how we learn to follow Jesus and produce good fruit that lasts.

Not surprisingly, Jesus went on to tell a parable about bearing fruit. Fig trees normally bear fruit every year, but this man had waited for three years and found no fruit on his tree. Aramaic-speaking rabbis told a story about a palm tree that did not bear fruit. In that story, when the owner was about to dig the tree up, the palm tree spoke to him and asked for one more year. The man refused, saying, "You miserable tree! You did not bear your own fruit, so how could you bear other fruit?" By contrast, the farmhand in Jesus' parable showed extraordinary patience and asked the owner to give the tree another year to bear fruit and then if it bore no fruit, cut it down. To help the tree, he dug around the roots to allow water and fertilizer to penetrate the soil.

God wants each of us to bear good fruit that lasts. Jesus is like the farmhand asking for another year, digging around our roots, giving us the fertilizer we need. Repentance is the way we receive those nutrients. Listening for Jesus' voice and then exercising the faith his Word produces by taking steps in obedience is how we bear good fruit. As an example, Jesus listened to his Father during the Sabbath service in the synagogue and set a woman free who was bent over by the burden of an oppressive spirit. The leader of the synagogue criticized Jesus for this amazing act of miraculous mercy, totally missing what it means to listen and respond to God's voice! Jesus called out the hypocrisy of supporting the untying of animals on the Sabbath but trying to prevent him from setting this precious woman free.

Are you bearing good fruit that lasts? If not, what does it mean for you to repent? How can you listen for the voice of Jesus and respond by exercising the faith he is planting in your heart one step at a time?

REFLECT AND RESPOND
What is Jesus saying to me right now?

What step of faith is Jesus calling me to take today?

DAY 54

READ AND LISTEN: LUKE 13:18-30
Take a minute to listen for what the Spirit is saying in these verses…

COMMENT AND CONSIDER

Jesus continued his long, slow journey to Jerusalem, but he was not in a hurry. His plan was to arrive in time for the Passover feast. In the meantime, Jesus moved from town to village, teaching the Good News of the Kingdom. As he made his way south, he told a simple parable about the mustard seed. Just as that tiny seed grows into something completely out of proportion to its size, so it is with the Kingdom.

Historically we can see this is true. Jesus was an unmarried builder from an obscure village in the backwaters of Galilee who gathered mostly blue-collar workers and everyday people and formed a movement of love and grace that literally changed the world! This is how the Kingdom works. Big things come from small things. Birds can nest in the branches of the tree that grows from a tiny mustard seed.

In the same way, a tiny amount of leaven mixed into sixty pounds of flour will eventually permeate the huge lump of dough. Just like yeast silently spreading through the dough, the Kingdom of God spreads from person to person, family to family, changing hearts and transforming lives, often without other people realizing it. Before you know it, the Good News has infiltrated everywhere!

We can also see this parable played out in history. These ordinary, everyday followers of Jesus demonstrated the love of God and shared the Good News of the Kingdom, so that life after life changed. Despite brutal persecution designed to stamp out this movement, the Kingdom of God continued to spread throughout the Roman Empire. By the time Emperor Constantine became a Christian in AD 312, over 55% of the people in the Roman Empire had become followers of Jesus! The Kingdom of God silently permeates all things, often without us realizing it, transforming the very order of things.

Luke records one of the many questions people asked Jesus, *"Lord, are only a few people going to be saved?"* This question was sometimes debated in first-century Judaism. Most Jews assumed all the people of Israel would be saved, as was recorded in the Mishnah, "All Israelites have a share in the world to come." (See Isaiah 60:21.) But others were not so sure, as we read in the first-century BC Jewish writing called 2 Esdras or 4 Ezra: "The Most High made this world for the sake of many, but the world to come for the sake of only a few... Many have been created, but only a few shall be saved."

Jesus responded by recalling the familiar image of a narrow door. Extended families lived in walled compounds made up of multiple rooms surrounding an open-air courtyard with porch roofs. This central courtyard gave access to all the rooms and was accessed through one very strong door that could be locked and barred to prevent bandits from breaking in. The wider a door was, the harder it was to secure and defend, so often these outer doors were just the width of a person. Once that door was locked and barred, there was no way to break it open and enter. Jesus said this is how it is in the Kingdom of God. The Kingdom is for everyone, but there is only one person through whom you can enter it. That is why Jesus referred to himself as *"the gate."* (John 10:7)

Jesus made it clear this narrow door was open for anyone willing to listen to his voice and follow in faith. But he also said that narrow door would not stand open forever. The day is coming when that door will be closed, and those who did not enter by faith will be excluded from the Kingdom. If we wait until that time to repent and pound on that door, we will have excluded ourselves from his Kingdom forever.

Do you act as if big Kingdom outcomes can grow from tiny steps of faith? How can you let the Kingdom of God permeate and transform your life like yeast? What does it mean for you to enter the narrow gate today and not put it off until tomorrow?

REFLECT AND RESPOND

What is Jesus saying to me right now?

What step of faith is Jesus calling me to take today?

Footsteps Every Week: Review

Write a brief summary of what Jesus said to you each day this past week and the step of faith he called you to take:

Monday

Tuesday

Wednesday

Thursday

Friday

Saturday

Footsteps Every Week: Reflect

Big Picture
As you look over what Jesus has said to you this past week, do you see any themes? What is the most important thing you need to remember and believe?

Predictable Pattern
As you look over what Jesus called you to do this past week, is there a new predictable pattern he is inviting you to establish in your life with God and others?

Plant the Word
As you look over the readings from this past week, write out the passage that feels most important for you and memorize it over the next week:

DAY 55

READ AND LISTEN: LUKE 13:31-14:6

Take a minute to listen for what the Spirit is saying in these verses…

COMMENT AND CONSIDER

Jesus had a complicated relationship with the religious leaders of his time. On the one hand, they were threatened by the indisputable authority of his teaching confirmed by his miraculous acts of power. The Pharisees, teachers of the Law in the local synagogues, were afraid Jesus' popularity and influence would reduce their own. Priests in the Jerusalem Temple were afraid he would undermine the power they wielded through the sacrificial system, especially after he turned over tables in the Temple courts.

On the other hand, some religious leaders were drawn to Jesus because of the very same teaching and authority that threatened others. They invited him to teach in their synagogues, listened carefully to his teaching, and hosted banquets in his honor. Although Jesus prophetically called out the hypocrisy and corruption of religious leaders, he did not reject or condemn them on the whole. Some Pharisees like Nicodemus, and eventually Saul of Tarsus, became followers of Jesus, as did *"a large group of priests."* (Acts 6:7) In this passage we read of a Pharisee who warned Jesus of Herod Antipas' plan to kill him, urging him to flee the Tetrarch's rule in Galilee.

Jesus' response to this warning demonstrates he did not operate from a position of fear the way so many of the religious leaders who were threatened by him did. Despite this legitimate threat to Jesus' well-being, he responded by calling the most powerful man in all of Galilee a *"fox"* and telling him to sit back and watch him work. A fox in first-century Palestine represented a voracious predator that preyed on the vulnerable and wrought destruction. Jesus made it clear he was not afraid or intimidated by Antipas and, although he was traveling south to Jerusalem, he was not fleeing Herod, but following the path the Father set out for him.

While Jesus was not afraid for himself, he knew how real the coming threat was for the people of Jerusalem. It is no coincidence that foxes prey on chicks and Jesus said to the people of Jerusalem, *"How often I wanted to gather your children together, as a hen gathers her chicks under her wings, but you were not willing!"* Jesus prophesied the very Psalm the crowds would quote when he entered Jerusalem over the Mount of Olives on Palm Sunday (Psalm 118:26). He also prophesied the terrible destruction that would befall Jerusalem some 40 years later when the Romans destroyed the Temple and burned the city.

Biblical prophets speak on behalf of God to his people, warning them, comforting them, and guiding them. Prophets also carry out provocative public acts to demonstrate what God is saying to his people. Here we see Jesus operating in the fullness of his calling as a prophet, warning the people and demonstrating the Kingdom by healing on the Sabbath. Pointing to the tragic history of prophets who were killed for their unpopular messages, he explained the reason for his journey to the Holy City by saying somewhat hyperbolically, *"because it is not possible for a prophet to perish outside of Jerusalem."*

We often think of Jesus in his role as a Teacher and as the Savior of humanity, but sometimes we forget he was also a Prophet. Not only are we to pay attention to how God is speaking to us through his words and his actions, but we are also to follow his example by learning to operate in the gift of prophecy rather than in fear and intimidation like the religious leaders. Paul makes it clear that prophecy did not end with the Old Testament prophets, John the Baptist, or Jesus, but that all those who follow Jesus and are filled with the Spirit can learn to operate in the prophetic. In fact, he says it is critical to the health of the body of Christ. (See 1 Corinthians 14.)

Are you receiving the prophetic word and example of Jesus in your life today? Are you learning how to speak and demonstrate God's message to the people around you? Those who listen for God's personal Word and share it with others will overcome fear and learn to walk more boldly by faith.

Reflect and Respond
What is Jesus saying to me right now?

What step of faith is Jesus calling me to take today?

DAY 56

READ AND LISTEN: LUKE 14:7-24

Take a minute to listen for what the Spirit is saying in these verses…

COMMENT AND CONSIDER

In the highly communal honor/shame culture of first-century Judaism, when you attended a banquet, your place at the table was a big deal. Most banquets were carried out around a low U-shaped table called a "triclinium," with the guests reclining on pillows around the outside of the table. The host sat in the second position on the left side of the U, with his spouse or co-host on his right and the guest of honor on his left. The seats continued in descending levels of honor as you moved away from the host, with the place of lowest honor on the far end of the table.

At a banquet in his honor, Jesus was seated on the left side of the table, just to the left of the hosts. The other guests tried to sit as close to Jesus as they could, vying for positions of greater honor. Jesus told them they should do exactly the opposite by purposely choosing a position of lower honor. If they chose the higher position, the host might humiliate them by making them move down the ladder of honor, but if they chose a position of humility, the host might call them up to a higher position of honor. This is a vivid illustration of Jesus' teaching, *"For everyone who exalts himself will be humbled, and the one who humbles himself will be exalted."*

Then Jesus addressed the motives of the Pharisee who was hosting the meal. If you hosted a meal attended by people of high social status, it brought great honor to you and your extended family. Jesus told his host not to invite people of status and means who could repay him in kind, but rather to invite people of lower social status and income. This would ensure he was not seeking his own benefit, but genuinely wanted to bless others, even those who could never repay his generosity.

All this talk of banquets caused one of the guests to exclaim, *"Blessed is the one who will eat bread in the kingdom of God!"* He was referring to Isaiah's prophecy of the coming messianic banquet, *"On this mountain, the Lord of Armies will prepare for all the peoples a feast of choice meat, a feast with aged wine, prime cuts of choice meat, fine vintage wine"* (Isaiah 25:6). Although Isaiah's vision clearly included the Gentiles (*"all the peoples"*), most first-century Jews assumed non-Jews would be excluded. Jesus took the opportunity to tell a parable of radical inclusion.

Typically, a host sent his servants out to invite people to a major banquet to be held on a certain day. Once he knew who was coming, he could decide how much meat to butcher for the feast. When all was ready for the banquet to start, the host sent out his servants a second time, telling the guests the banquet was ready and summoning them to come and enjoy. In Jesus' story the leading members of society were invited and accepted the invitation. When the feast was ready, the servants went back out to summon the guests, but they all came up with obviously fake excuses for canceling. In addition to the massive social insult of this last-minute snub, this also left the host with a large financial loss as the food could not be preserved and would go to waste.

Shockingly, the host ordered his servants, *"Go out quickly into the streets and alleys of the city, and bring in here the poor, maimed, blind, and lame."* Then he sent them out a second time to gather up the outcasts who were even further afield to make sure the banquet was full and nothing would go to waste. Jesus was making a clear statement: the entitled and self-righteous were the ones snubbing God, and God responded by inviting the social and religious outcasts to be part of his Kingdom. The elite became outcasts, and the outcasts became honored guests.

Will you join Jesus at the banquet or snub his generosity with your weak excuses? Who will you invite to join you?

Reflect and Respond
What is Jesus saying to me right now?

What step of faith is Jesus calling me to take today?

DAY 57

READ AND LISTEN: LUKE 14:25-35

Take a minute to listen for what the Spirit is saying in these verses…

COMMENT AND CONSIDER

Jesus told the rich young ruler one of the most important laws is *"honor your father and mother."* (Luke 18:20) But in this passage, he says anyone who wants to follow him has to *"hate his own father and mother, wife and children, brothers and sisters."* Likewise, he said one of the greatest commandments is to love *"your neighbor as yourself."* (Luke 10:27) But here he says to be a disciple, we have to hate our own life. What does Jesus mean by these harsh and seemingly contradictory statements?

Jesus was being crystal clear about the cost of following him. As he said, it would be stupid to begin building a watchtower to guard your vineyard only to discover you didn't have enough stones to finish it. In an honor/shame culture where public ridicule was one of the worst things that could happen to you, an unfinished tower on your property would be a continual monument to your foolishness! Likewise, it would be sheer folly to lead your army into battle without considering whether you actually had the resources to overcome your enemy. History is full of tragic examples of leaders who failed to do this and paid the price. Jesus' point is that we should carefully consider what is required to be his disciple before we sign up to follow him.

In first-century Judaism, discipleship was a special relationship between a follower and his teacher. Most boys finished their elementary education in *Beth Sefer* (Hebrew for "House of the Book") by the age of 12, then left to learn the family business. The best students applied to continue their studies in *Beth Midrash* ("House of Interpretation") from roughly the age of 12 to 18. These students could become scribes who wrote up legal contracts and other documents. The best of these students applied directly to the rabbi and, if accepted, became one of his disciples (*Beth Talmid*: "House of the Learner"). These disciples moved in with the rabbi, lived as part of his extended family, listened to his words, imitated his way of life, and eventually became rabbis themselves.

Jesus, who was not formally trained as a rabbi, turned this process upside down by initiating the invitation for people to follow him. He called everyday people who would never dream of applying to become a disciple of the rabbi. That would be like a high school dropout applying to Harvard Law School! The result was a houseful of people from a broad range of backgrounds who answered the call to follow Jesus. Twelve of them agreed to leave their jobs and follow Jesus full-time, but the whole housefull was called "disciples." (See Matthew 12:46-50.)

Now Jesus made it clear that to be his disciple, following him needs to become your highest commitment, higher than your commitment to natural family, higher than your commitment to financial success, higher even than your commitment to self-preservation. This is why the ultimate symbol of Jesus-shaped discipleship is the willingness to take up your cross. We must be willing to put to death anything in our lives that would keep us from following him. He told the rich young ruler to sell all his possessions and give the money to the poor, because he knew that man's wealth was his highest commitment. (See Luke 18:22.) He told the man whose father had died to let others bury him. (See Luke 9:59-60.) He told Peter that one day he would be executed on a cross just like his Rabbi. (See John 21:18-19.)

To *"hate"* your father and mother, your brothers and sisters, even your own life, simply means that even the most important relationships in your life must become less important than your relationship with Jesus if you are going to be his disciple. What is most important in your life? What is your highest commitment? Are you willing to put following Jesus before every other thing in your life? If so, then you are becoming his disciple.

REFLECT AND RESPOND

What is Jesus saying to me right now?

What step of faith is Jesus calling me to take today?

DAY 58

READ AND LISTEN: LUKE 15:1-10

Take a minute to listen for what the Spirit is saying in these verses…

COMMENT AND CONSIDER

The scribes and Pharisees developed a strictly compartmentalized worldview in which people were either in or out. This was partly based on the highly legalistic culture they developed in which a person's standing before God was based on their ability to obey not only the biblical laws of the Old Testament, but also myriad rules and rituals the rabbis had developed. It was also based on the categories of clean and unclean that developed from the symbolic purity laws governing what you could eat and touch. These religious leaders labeled entire groups of people as unclean based on their purity rules and the assumptions made about that group.

For instance, shepherding flocks has a long history as a humble but noble profession in the Bible, especially since King David was once a shepherd boy. God is often referred to as the ideal shepherd, and the leaders of Israel were sometimes compared to shepherds who had shirked their responsibilities. However, the Pharisees decided, due to the long months shepherds spent far from home watching over their flocks, shepherds should generally be considered unclean because they were obviously unable to follow all the religious rules and rituals which the Pharisees had imposed on the people.

This habit of labeling people unclean based on life circumstances or assumptions resulted in many people feeling unjustly condemned and rejected. It is no wonder so many wanted nothing to do with this kind of judgmental and ritualized religion! Jesus, on the other hand, welcomed people unconditionally, told people of a God who loved them regardless of their category, and demonstrated this love in concrete action. Of course the outcasts flocked to him! As Luke says, *"All the tax collectors and sinners were approaching to listen to him."* When the Pharisees complained about Jesus welcoming and eating with these so-called *"sinners,"* he told a series of parables about God's orientation to those outside their category of religious acceptability.

In the first story, Jesus told of a shepherd who led his flocks far from home to find green pasture but lost one of his sheep. A flock of one hundred sheep was average for a family of modest means and took more than one person to tend. One lost sheep represented only a 1% loss, yet the shepherd left the 99 sheep in the care of the other shepherds to search until he found the lost sheep. When he found it, he didn't punish the lost sheep but joyfully put it over his shoulders and led the other sheep and shepherd home for a celebration!

Likewise, a woman saved up ten silver coins, each worth about a day's wages—a significant amount for the financially oppressed peasants of Galilee. When she lost one of the coins in her house, she carefully swept the floor until she found it. Houses in first-century Palestine often had floors made of uncut stones, creating many deep crevices where a small coin could go unnoticed. Perhaps by sweeping she hoped to hear it clinking against the stones. When she finally found the coin, she invited her friends and neighbors to rejoice with her because what was lost had been found.

To people who were used to being condemned and rejected, these stories were like cold water to the thirsty. Hearing that God valued them so much he would search for them until he found them was a powerful message of grace. Being joyfully celebrated rather than harshly reprimanded was music to their ears. This is what Good News sounds like! After inviting himself to stay with Zacchaeus, the chief tax collector of Jericho, Jesus said, *"the Son of Man has come to seek and to save the lost."* (Luke 19:10)

What is your attitude toward those outside your religious circles? Are you as concerned about lost people as this shepherd and woman were about what they had lost? How are you seeking to find people who are lost?

Reflect and Respond

What is Jesus saying to me right now?

What step of faith is Jesus calling me to take today?

DAY 59

READ AND LISTEN: LUKE 15:11-32

Take a minute to listen for what the Spirit is saying in these verses…

COMMENT AND CONSIDER

Jesus told a story about a man who had two sons. When the younger son demanded his portion of the inheritance (one-third of all the family's property and assets), it was as if he were saying "Father, I wish you were dead!" Jesus' hearers would have expected the father to beat his son for such an insult, or worse. The same chapter of Deuteronomy that stipulates the division of property between sons also calls for parents to bring their rebellious sons to the village elders to be stoned to death. (See Deuteronomy 21:18-21.) But shockingly the father agreed to the outrageous demand of this insolent son and gave him one-third of everything.

Middle Eastern farmers do not live out in isolated homes in the middle of their farmland. They live in the village and go out to their plot of land surrounding the village to till, plant, and harvest. That means all of this is not happening in private isolation; instead, the whole village would be aware of what this son did. In an honor/shame culture, that meant, by letting the son take his inheritance early and sell it, the father allowed the son to humiliate him before the entire village.

The younger son headed to a Gentile city where he squandered his father's life savings on wild and immoral living. Not surprisingly the money soon ran out, and the son was reduced to feeding pigs, considered unclean by Jewish religious standards. The Talmud says, "Cursed is the man who raises swine." The cursed son was even jealous of these unclean pigs, hungry for the slop he was feeding them! The pig feed was carob pods which were eaten only by the poorest people.

A rabbinic saying reads: "When the Israelites are reduced to eating carob pods, then they repent." And that is exactly what happened: *"he came to himself."* Realizing his father's workers were better off than him, the younger son decided to return home. He knew restoration as a member of the extended family was out of the question, but he hoped his father would be gracious enough to accept him back as an employee. So he began to prepare his confession speech.

Contrary to western culture, in the Middle East it is considered improper for a man of means to hurry in public. Only the poor had to hurry in order to make enough money to eat; people of honorable position could take their time because they had all the time in the world. However, when the father saw his son at a distance, he was so overjoyed he threw caution to the wind and ran through the village to meet him. Now the father humiliated himself before the very same villagers who heaped shame on him for letting his rebellious son go in the first place.

The son assumed the father was running to rebuke him and beat him, so he quickly launched into his repentant speech, but the father was not interested in that. Interrupting his son, he clothed him in his own robe and put the ring of authority on his finger and shoes on his battered feet, symbolizing his restoration to sonship, not slavery. The father ordered a calf slaughtered for a feast to celebrate his son's return, which meant he was inviting the entire village to the party! It is impossible to imagine a more unexpected or gracious response from the father.

However, the older son was deeply resentful of this lavish display of forgiveness toward his rebellious brother and refused to come into the party. Now he was the one publicly shaming his father before the entire village by refusing to participate. Again, the father shamed himself by coming out to the older son, assuring him of his own inheritance, and begging him to celebrate his brother's return from the dead. Then Jesus leaves the story unfinished. Where do you find yourself in this story? Are you the rebellious son or the welcoming father or the self-righteous son? How will you finish the story?

Reflect and Respond

What is Jesus saying to me right now?

What step of faith is Jesus calling me to take today?

DAY 60

READ AND LISTEN: LUKE 16:1-18

Take a minute to listen for what the Spirit is saying in these verses...

COMMENT AND CONSIDER

Nearly everyone in the first century lived in an extended family (Greek: *oikos*) if they could. These families, made up of both blood and non-blood relationships, centered around a family business. There were farming families, fishing families, shepherds, builders, potters, leatherworkers, weavers, and so on. If a family's business became successful, they could afford to hire a manager to run the business and free up the members of the family to enjoy their success. The Greek word for manager is *oikonomos,* which literally means "the ruler of the extended family." Those who employed a trustworthy and competent manager were free to leave the family business in his hands and travel.

Jesus tells a story of a rich man who had a manager to run his successful family business. However, he received a credible tip that this man was mismanaging his business. The manager *"squandered"* his master's property. This is the same verb used to describe the prodigal son's actions (Luke 15:13). So the owner of the family business called in his manager and demanded an accounting of the books before he fired the manager. The manager realized he would soon be out of a job, knew he was not cut out for manual labor, and couldn't stomach the thought of having to beg, so he devised a plan. He drastically reduced the debts of some of the wealthy men who owed his master significant amounts of capital, gaining powerful friends who now owed him a favor. This meant that once he was out of a job, he would have places to stay and influential people who would help him.

Jesus' parables often have a surprising twist ending, and this one is no exception. Everyone listening to Jesus expected the master to explode in rage and condemn the manager when he found out what he had done. Instead, the master praised the dishonest manager. Why would the master praise him? The answer to this question is the point of the parable.

This is one of the most difficult of Jesus' parables for many people to understand because it seems as though Jesus is affirming an irresponsible manager who acted dishonestly to serve his own interests. It is important to remember that parables are not moral allegories with direct symbolic associations. They are stories based in real life that make a point illustrating the Kingdom of God. Jesus is not telling us to dishonestly seek our own advantage; he is showing us something about living in God's Kingdom.

In Middle Eastern culture, we find a genre of stories about clever people who gain an advantage over powerful people by acting shrewdly. People love to hear about the resourceful underdog who triumphs over the powerful and often laugh at how they pulled it off. This is one of those kinds of stories, and people probably laughed when they heard the master praising the manager who tricked him! The reason the owner affirmed the manager was not for his dishonesty or his self-serving actions, but rather for the shrewdness he displayed in adapting to his crisis and ensuring his future security.

Here Jesus was using the familiar rabbinic method of teaching called *qal wahomer,* meaning "from light to heavy." If something is true in this light situation, how much more is it true in this heavy situation? If an incompetent, self-serving manager could be this clever in using the available resources to ensure his future, how much more should *"the children of light"* be clever in leveraging their capitals to advance the Kingdom of God? Of course, this does not mean we are to be dishonest or self-serving, but it does mean we are to be careful and wise with what has been entrusted to us and find creative ways to advance God's purposes, even through worldly resources. Jesus is clear in stating, *"You cannot serve both God and money."*

What resources has God entrusted to you? How are you managing those capitals? Are there creative ways you can leverage what you have to advance the Kingdom?

REFLECT AND RESPOND

What is Jesus saying to me right now?

What step of faith is Jesus calling me to take today?

FOOTSTEPS EVERY WEEK: REVIEW

Write a brief summary of what Jesus said to you each day this past week and the step of faith he called you to take:

Monday

Tuesday

Wednesday

Thursday

Friday

Saturday

Footsteps Every Week: Reflect

Big Picture
As you look over what Jesus has said to you this past week, do you see any themes? What is the most important thing you need to remember and believe?

Predictable Pattern
As you look over what Jesus called you to do this past week, is there a new predictable pattern he is inviting you to establish in your life with God and others?

Plant the Word
As you look over the readings from this past week, write out the passage that feels most important for you and memorize it over the next week:

DAY 61

READ AND LISTEN: LUKE 16:19-31

Take a minute to listen for what the Spirit is saying in these verses…

COMMENT AND CONSIDER

First-century Judaism had a tendency to associate wealth with God's favor and blessing, while interpreting poverty as God's judgment and rejection. The assumption was wealthy people must be doing something right, while those in need clearly had failed in some way. In the modern West we find a parallel supposition that rich people have worked hard to earn their success and deserve to enjoy it, while poor people are lazy and irresponsible and deserve to suffer as a result. However, Jesus gives us a very different perspective on wealth and poverty. He is most critical of those who use their positions of power to enrich themselves at the expense of others, while welcoming the poor and outcast, calling them *"blessed."* (See Luke 6:20.)

Purple robes were extremely expensive because the dye used to attain that color came from thousands of murex sea snails, each providing just one drop of ink. Linen was a soft, smooth fabric woven from flax fibers and was used for the most expensive undergarments. A modern equivalent to being clothed in *"purple and fine linen"* would be furs and silk. In first-century Palestine, most people ate bread, dates, and olives, only enjoying meat on holidays and for special occasions. However, this man dined at lavish banquets every day.

A number of homes owned by wealthy families from this period have been excavated, and they all contain many rooms, built around a central courtyard accessed by a strong, exterior gate that could be securely locked. At the outer gate of this rich man's house a man named Lazarus, impoverished by his sickness, lay in hope that he could eat some of the scraps which fell to the ground from this family's table. Each day, as he came and went from his large home, the rich man ignored Lazarus, not even bothering to give him his trash to pick through. Instead, dogs, considered dangerous and unclean in Middle Eastern culture, paid attention to Lazarus by licking his sores.

Before long Lazarus succumbed to his illness and the poverty that prevented his treatment and was taken to *"Abraham's side"* (literally: "to the fold of Abraham's robe"). This is an allusion to the great Messianic banquet foretold by the prophets in which we will join with all the saints of the ages in an eternal celebration of the Messiah's triumph over sin, death, hell, and the devil. The picture here is of Lazarus reclining on a pillow at that great banquet, in a position of honor, leaning back on Abraham's chest as they enjoy the meal together. (See John 13:23 for a parallel.)

Despite the advantages of his wealth, the rich man also died, but he was taken to Hades, the place where the wicked dead are punished. From his fiery torment, he saw Father Abraham far away, dining with the Messiah and Lazarus at his side. He cried out for Abraham to send Lazarus to drip even a drop of cool water on his tongue. But Abraham pointed out the justice of this radical reversal and the impossibility of changing the outcome after death. When the rich man asked that at least Lazarus be sent to his extended family to warn them of the consequences of their injustice, Abraham pointed out they had already read the demands for justice from the Law and the Prophets, and even someone rising from the dead would not change their minds, a clear allusion to Jesus' impending resurrection.

Jesus was crystal clear that his coming Kingdom will turn our worldly social order upside down. As he said, *"Some who are last will be first, and some who are first will be last."* (Luke 13:30) For those of us who are relatively rich in comparison to most of the world's population, this is a sobering wake-up call urging us consider what it means to do justice, love mercy, and care for the vulnerable among us today. Who is lying outside your gate that you have not even noticed? What does the Kingdom look like in that situation?

REFLECT AND RESPOND

What is Jesus saying to me right now?

What step of faith is Jesus calling me to take today?

DAY 62

READ AND LISTEN: LUKE 17:1-10

Take a minute to listen for what the Spirit is saying in these verses…

COMMENT AND CONSIDER

Self-righteousness is the belief that we can make ourselves right with God through our own moral effort and religious rituals. This leads to an attitude of entitlement which grows from the assumption that we deserve credit for what we have done. We start to believe we have earned a status superior to those who do not follow our moral code or religious practices. This, in turn, leads to condescension and judgment toward those who do not live up to our perceived standards. This is precisely the posture of many religious leaders at the time of Jesus, especially the Pharisees.

Jesus was adamantly opposed to this posture of self-righteousness and entitlement. He taught an extremely high moral standard, such as *"love your enemies and pray for those who persecute you… Be perfect, therefore, as your heavenly Father is perfect"* (Matthew 5:44, 48). But Jesus was clear this rigorous morality would never come from our efforts to change ourselves because we cannot earn God's acceptance. (See the parable of the workers in the vineyard, Matthew 20:1-16.) He showed us real change must start with the transformation of our hearts and minds, not from external rituals or moral willpower. (See Mark 7:14-23.)

The Good News of the Kingdom is that we are forgiven and accepted as a gift of grace received by faith in Jesus. As we learn to trust him, God's Spirit changes our hearts and minds, filling us with his love that overflows in acts of love and mercy toward others. This is what allows us to follow in Jesus' footsteps and live a more Jesus-shaped life. Whatever good fruit comes from our lives is a gift for which we cannot take credit because we did not earn it!

In this passage Jesus addressed the self-righteous attitude of the religious leaders who caused offense by their glaring hypocrisy. Jesus focused his ministry on those who were judged and rejected by the Pharisees. It was these *"little ones"* for whose stumbling they were liable. When visiting the places where Jesus taught, we often see huge basalt millstones used to crush olives, weighing tons. If you were thrown into a lake with one of these tied around your neck, you would never be seen again!

In contrast to the judgmentalism of these hypercritical religious leaders, Jesus told his followers to freely forgive even those who sin against you repeatedly. This is reminiscent of Jesus' parable in which the man who was just forgiven billions of dollars of debt refused to forgive the man who owed him a few hundred dollars. (See Matthew 18:21-35.) It is precisely God's grace toward us that empowers us to show grace to one another. But notice, Jesus also tells us to hold each other accountable for our actions and call each other to repentance by confronting sin.

When the disciples felt the challenge of these teachings, they exclaimed, *"Increase our faith."* Jesus responded by pointing out they did not need more faith; they simply needed to exercise the mustard seed-sized faith they already had! He told them a simple story illustrating the right attitude of a sinner saved by grace. No servant coming back to the house after a long day of work would ever imagine he had earned the right to sit back and relax while the master served him. And yet, this was exactly the posture of the Pharisees.

Instead, Jesus told us to take the posture of a servant who has not earned special privileges or status by our efforts but who has simply done what we were assigned. Jesus said the mindset we should adopt when we have done all that we were commanded is, *"We are unworthy servants; we've only done our duty."* This is the perspective of those who know they have been given a gift they could never earn and is too great to repay, a gift that can only be accepted in a spirit of humble gratitude.

When you serve God and others, what is your attitude? Can you identify subtle ways that self-righteousness is creeping into your heart and mind? Are you exercising whatever amount of faith you have today?

REFLECT AND RESPOND

What is Jesus saying to me right now?

What step of faith is Jesus calling me to take today?

DAY 63

READ AND LISTEN: LUKE 17:11-19

Take a minute to listen for what the Spirit is saying in these verses…

COMMENT AND CONSIDER

People afflicted with visible skin lesions caused by psoriasis, lupus, ringworm, and other afflictions are called "lepers" in the Bible, but this is not Hansen's Disease, which is what we call leprosy today. Those who contracted such skin conditions were forced to separate from their family and community and cry out "Unclean! Unclean" whenever someone approached them. (See Leviticus 13:45-46.) As a result of this forced exile from society, lepers often banded together to survive. The fact that these ten lepers included a Samaritan demonstrates how desperate they were for community.

The Samaritans were the descendants of the Israelites of the northern ten tribes who were conquered by the Assyrians in the eighth century BC and intermarried with them. Jews who descended from the two tribes of the southern kingdom considered these Samaritans to be racially impure religious heretics because they did not worship at the Temple in Jerusalem or follow the teachings of the Writings and the Prophets. As a result, they minimized contact with Samaritans as much as possible, assuming they were unclean, dishonest, and untrustworthy.

As Jesus and the disciples continued their journey to Jerusalem, they passed from Galilee into Samaria. There they encountered this small colony of ten lepers who lived on the outskirts of a village. Carefully following the Levitical commands, they stood at a distance from Jesus, identified themselves as lepers, and cried out to Jesus for healing. Apparently, Jesus did not approach these afflicted people to touch and heal them as they had hoped, but simply told them, *"Go and show yourselves to the priests."* These lepers must have wondered why Jesus was sending them to the priest to be declared clean when they still exhibited all the signs of their disease. But they decided to trust Jesus and went anyway.

Luke the Physician tells us that *"while they were going, they were cleansed."* Imagine their excitement as the rashes and lesions disappeared from their arms and legs while they walked along the road! No longer would they be ostracized from their communities. They could return to their spouses and their children and their family business. In their joy and wonder, they forgot all about who had healed them. Except for one. That one was the Samaritan. He returned to Jesus, giving glory to God and falling face down at Jesus' feet, thanking him for this amazing gift.

Jesus sometimes made a Samaritan the hero of his stories, much to the surprise of his mostly Jewish audience. But here was a real-life example of a Samaritan breaking the racist stereotypes in demonstrating gratitude to Jesus for all he did for him. As Jesus said, *"Were not ten cleansed? Where are the nine? Didn't any return to give glory to God except this foreigner? ... Get up and go on your way. Your faith has saved you."* They were all saved by grace through faith, but only one of them recognized the gift Jesus had given and expressed his thanks.

Gratitude is the recognition that we have received something we do not deserve. We are not grateful for our wages because we worked to earn them. It is a gift that evokes gratitude. Recognizing that all we are and all we have is a gift from God nurtures an attitude of gratitude. When we give thanks to Jesus for saving us and giving us far more than we could ever deserve, we begin to experience the joy of the gift we have received. This is why worship is so powerful. Recognizing God as good and as the Giver of every good thing in our life multiplies the fruit of joy, which moves us to acts of goodness and kindness toward others.

Are you willing to trust Jesus and act on his word even if you don't see the results immediately? Do you recognize God as the source of every good thing in your life? When was the last time you genuinely gave thanks to Jesus for all he has done for you?

Reflect and Respond

What is Jesus saying to me right now?

What step of faith is Jesus calling me to take today?

DAY 64

READ AND LISTEN: LUKE 17:20-37

Take a minute to listen for what the Spirit is saying in these verses…

COMMENT AND CONSIDER

Jews had different expectations about the coming of the Messiah at the time of Jesus, but the predominant view was a political and militaristic one. The Pharisees were the leading proponents of the expectation that the Messiah would come as an anointed Davidic ruler and would dramatically lead God's people in armed revolt against the Romans and all the Gentiles to establish a new government to rule Israel and the world according to the will of God. The so-called *Psalms of Solomon*, written by Pharisees shortly before the time of Jesus, beg God to raise up the Messiah to rule over Israel, destroy her enemies, and finally establish his rule over the earth. When we read the Old Testament Prophets, it is easy to understand why the Pharisees developed this kind of Messianic expectation, because many prophecies foretell the cataclysmic events in which God will once and for all establish his rule over the whole world.

However, other prophecies were overlooked and are still avoided in many Jewish circles, which describe another event. Isaiah 53 tells of a humble servant who would come to suffer and willingly lay down his life on behalf of God's people. Isaiah prophesied, *"he was pierced because of our rebellion, crushed because of our iniquities; punishment for our peace was on him, and we are healed by his wounds. We all went astray like sheep; we all have turned to our own way; and the Lord has punished him for the iniquity of us all."* (Isaiah 53:5, 6) This description is very different from the image of a royal Messiah coming in glory to conquer evil and establish God's rule.

Since Jesus constantly taught about the Kingdom of God, the Pharisees wanted to know when the dramatic political and military action was going to start. But Jesus told them the Kingdom would not begin with observable events such as armed conflict between the armies of Israel and Rome or the establishment of a new government in the Palace of Herod in Jerusalem.

Instead, he said, *"the kingdom of God is in your midst."* In an individualistic culture like the modern west, it is easy to internalize this passage and think of the Kingdom as something that happens "in your heart." But in a more communal culture, like that of the Middle East, it is clear Jesus is describing a Kingdom that begins in relationships among people in community.

Jesus warned us people would try to start a dramatic conflict in the name of the Messiah. In fact, a number of such failed "messiahs" lived the first century, including Theudas, Judah the Galilean, or the Egyptian and the Assassins. (See Acts 5:36-37; 21:38.) In each of these cases, the Roman army brutally destroyed the messianic pretenders and those who followed them. Jesus told us to take a skeptical stance toward those who try to bring God's Kingdom coercively through political and military means. *"Don't follow or run after them."* Instead, Jesus said of the Messiah, *"first it is necessary that he suffer many things and be rejected by this generation."*

But Jesus went on to say that the Son of Man would return in a dramatic event of cosmic proportions. This unexpected but unmistakable cataclysmic event will be as obvious as flashes of lightning that illuminate the entire sky! He compared this second coming to the biblical accounts of the global flood in the time of Noah and the heavenly conflagration of Sodom in the time of Lot, both of which came suddenly with swift justice. Jesus said when this happens, there won't be time to come downstairs from your rooftop or return to your home from working in the fields. Some people will remain as part of this new, fully realized Kingdom of God, and others who rejected it will be suddenly removed.

Do you know the difference between Jesus' first coming and his return? How is the Kingdom coming among you and the people you know? How can you live today so that when Jesus suddenly returns you will be ready?

Reflect and Respond

What is Jesus saying to me right now?

What step of faith is Jesus calling me to take today?

DAY 65

READ AND LISTEN: LUKE 18:1-8

Take a minute to listen for what the Spirit is saying in these verses…

COMMENT AND CONSIDER

Jesus' extraordinary life flowed from his deep connection in prayer with his Father and the insights into the Father's will that came from that prayer life. He said, *"Truly I tell you, the Son is not able to do anything on his own, but only what he sees the Father doing. For whatever the Father does, the Son likewise does these things."* (John 5:19) As Jesus prepared his disciples for the challenging and stressful events which were coming, he told them a parable about prayer.

In Jesus' time judges were rabbis ordained by their own rabbi or the Sanhedrin to mediate between parties in conflict based on the Old Testament Law. The Gospels referred to these as the *"scribes"* and *"experts in the law."*. The parties in a civic dispute paid a rabbinical judge to consider the case they brought before him. After hearing the relevant evidence, the judge cited the Law and various rabbinical interpretations before ruling in the case. Judges were required to be wise, impartial, and just and were among the most powerful and influential members of society.

By contrast, widows were widely recognized as the most vulnerable members of society. Because most women could not carry out business or represent themselves without a father or husband, a woman left without a representative male in her life was subject to all kinds of oppression and victimization at the hands of unscrupulous men. The widow in this story had suffered some kind of injustice and had very little social capital to demand justice from her adversary. Her only recourse was to go to an impartial and just rabbi who might rule on her behalf.

However, in Jesus' story, the judge in question is neither impartial nor just. As Jesus said, he *"didn't fear God or respect people."* As a result, even though she had a valid claim in her case, the judge refuses to rule on her behalf. We can assume her adversary was offering bribes or special privileges under the table to secure the judge's ruling. What recourse does the widow have? She doesn't have influential friends who can convince the judge. She doesn't have enough money for a bribe. What she does have is perseverance. She keeps coming back to the judge day after day, demanding that he rule according to the clear intent of the Law.

Her persistence begins to draw the attention of the wider community. People are talking about her case. The judge starts to hear grumblings about his clear refusal to follow the Law in his rulings. Finally, the judge realizes he must follow the law and rule on her behalf if he is to maintain his standing in society and get on with his life! As he says, *"because this widow keeps pestering me, I will give her justice, so that she doesn't wear me out by her persistent coming."* Here Jesus was using the rabbinical approach *qal wahomer*, "light to heavy." He pointed out that if an unjust judge will finally cave in and give justice to a poor widow, how much more will God, who is perfectly just and righteous, give what is good and right to his own children when they *"cry out to him day and night."*

We should be careful not to think this parable is about us convincing a stingy and resistant God to do what we want him to do. That is the very opposite of what prayer is about! Prayer is meant to bring us into alignment with God's will so we become more effective conduits and agents of his Kingdom coming. His point is that persistence in this kind of submitted, Kingdom-seeking prayer is what brings the breakthrough of God's will being done on earth as it is in heaven.

Are you praying according to God's will or according to your own desires? Are you willing to seek God's will persistently until you see the Kingdom break through?

REFLECT AND RESPOND

What is Jesus saying to me right now?

What step of faith is Jesus calling me to take today?

DAY 66

READ AND LISTEN: LUKE 18:9-17
Take a minute to listen for what the Spirit is saying in these verses…

COMMENT AND CONSIDER
Although Jesus was quite critical of their legalism and hypocrisy, most Pharisees in the time of Jesus were admired by Jews for their learning and piety. Many people were critical of the Sadducees for their political alignment with the Romans and Herodians. Essenes were thought of as esoteric and irrelevant due to their isolated holiness. Zealots were considered highly religious, but also capricious and violent in exacting what they perceived to be God's justice.

By contrast, the Pharisees were legendary for their devotion to the Law of God and their meticulous application of that Law to the lives of everyday people. These rabbis preached the Law in the synagogue on the Sabbath, taught their children during the week in school, and fearlessly criticized the Herodians as traitors and the Sadducees as frauds. Many assumed the Pharisees were the ideal role models they should emulate.

Tax collectors were at the opposite end of the social and religious spectrum. As much as the Pharisees were admired and emulated, tax collectors were despised and hated. Like the Herodians, they worked for the Romans, but their betrayal was far more personal because they used threats of violence to extract unreasonable tax payments from struggling peasants. To make matters worse, they forced people to pay even more than was required to line their own pockets. The Pharisees taught that tax collectors were so unclean their entrance into a house rendered everything in it unclean. They would not accept donations for the poor from a tax collector and considered the presence of a tax collector in the Temple a defilement of the holy precincts. When Jesus began his parable, people would have automatically assumed the Pharisee is the hero of the story and the tax collector the villain.

The listeners would have assumed the tax collector's presence at the Temple was motivated by personal gain and the Pharisee's by piety. Fasting was only required on Yom Kippur, the Day of Atonement, but pious Jews, like this Pharisee, fasted on Mondays and Thursdays. The Pharisee's self-congratulatory prayer might have sounded familiar to Jesus' listeners. The Talmud attributes the following prayer to a first-century rabbi: "I give thanks before thee O Lord my God, and God of my fathers, that thou has appointed my portion with those who sit in the College and the Synagogue, and hast not appointed my lot in the theaters and circuses... I labor to inherit Paradise and they labor to inherit the pit of destruction."

But when Jesus began to quote the tax collector's prayer, it caught everyone listening by surprise. This tax collector is sorrowful for his treason and extortion. He assumes a position of humility before God. He beats his chest in a sign of genuine repentance. He is not trying to explain away or justify his actions. His prayer is honest, simple, and to the point: *"God, have mercy on me, a sinner!"* Shockingly, this humble and contrite man is the hero of the story, not the Pharisee! The hated tax collector's prayer is a model for our prayer life. As Jesus concluded, *"I tell you, this one went down to his house justified rather than the other, because everyone who exalts himself will be humbled, but the one who humbles himself will be exalted."*

As if to drive the point home, Luke records Jesus' countercultural act in welcoming and blessing the children. Lifting up a child as the role model for entering the Kingdom was almost as shocking as pointing to a tax collector as the role model for prayer! The Pharisee assumed his religious and moral efforts afforded him special status before God. The tax collector knew he was utterly dependent on God's grace and sorely in need of his mercy. What is your posture when you come to God in prayer? When was the last time you confessed your need for his mercy? How can you learn to come to Jesus as a little child?

Reflect and Respond

What is Jesus saying to me right now?

What step of faith is Jesus calling me to take today?

Footsteps Every Week: Review

Write a brief summary of what Jesus said to you each day this past week and the step of faith he called you to take:

Monday

Tuesday

Wednesday

Thursday

Friday

Saturday

Footsteps Every Week: Reflect

Big Picture
As you look over what Jesus has said to you this past week, do you see any themes? What is the most important thing you need to remember and believe?

Predictable Pattern
As you look over what Jesus called you to do this past week, is there a new predictable pattern he is inviting you to establish in your life with God and others?

Plant the Word
As you look over the readings from this past week, write out the passage that feels most important for you and memorize it over the next week:

DAY 67

READ AND LISTEN: LUKE 18:18-30

Take a minute to listen for what the Spirit is saying in these verses…

COMMENT AND CONSIDER

From the very beginning, the Bible is clear that God is good. The pagan world was filled with capricious gods who sometimes did good things and sometimes did bad things. But God created all things good, and human beings, created in his image, were deemed *"very good."* (Genesis 1:31) The goodness of this creation and us as creatures was compromised when the first human beings decided they could rule themselves independently of God. Sin entered them and their world, and the tragic results have played out in our lives ever since.

In light of this biblical worldview, the rabbis of the first century often debated what constituted the good life and what would ensure eternal participation in the fully redeemed creation when it finally attained the potential for good that Adam and Eve squandered. (See Luke 10:25.) We don't know what kind of ruler it was who posed this question to Jesus, but he was probably an official in Herod's court, since a synagogue ruler would most likely be identified with the scribes and Pharisees. Matthew tells us not only was he rich, but he was young. (See Matthew 19:20.)

Jesus immediately confronted this man's assumptions about what constitutes goodness. The young ruler's response tells us he believed goodness was a result of obeying the commands. It was common for religious Jews to assume that, if they could avoid overtly breaking any of the key commands of God, they were righteous by the standards of the Law. Saul the Pharisee believed he was *"regarding the righteousness that is in the law, blameless."* (Philippians 3:6) But Jesus made it clear that God is the only standard of true goodness, and no one measures up to that, even the most diligent followers of the Law. (See Matthew 5:48.)

Instead, Jesus defined goodness in relationship to himself. To be righteous is to be rightly related to God and those around us so that not only our external actions, but also our internal attitudes more and more reflect the absolute goodness of God. Jesus came to lead us into this kind of relationship with God, but it requires us to put our relationship with him before anything else in our lives. Jesus perceived that this young man's wealth took first place in his heart, and he knew the only way this ruler would enter the Kingdom of God was by giving away all his possessions. This would set him free to make following Jesus his first and highest commitment. As Jesus said, *"You still lack one thing: Sell all you have and distribute it to the poor, and you will have treasure in heaven. Then come, follow me."*

The ruler's extreme sadness confirmed Jesus' diagnosis; he did love his possessions more than anything else. To describe the depth of our attachment to money, Jesus used the fantastical comparison of a camel, the largest land animal in first-century Palestine, going through the eye of a needle, the smallest opening imaginable. Some have tried to soften this statement by connecting it to a small gate in the walls of Jerusalem that required a camel to get down on its knees to enter, but this is first attested to in the Crusader period, some thousand years after Jesus.

Returning to the ruler's original question of eternal life, some asked how anyone could be saved. Jesus' point was clear: *"What is impossible with man is possible with God."* Then, as usual, Peter spoke up and expressed what many of the disciples may have been feeling. They had left their family businesses, given up financial security, and were away from their families for weeks at a time while on mission with Jesus. What would they be left with in the end? Jesus assured them they would receive far more than they sacrificed, both in this life and in the life to come!

What is most important in your life? What are you willing to give up to follow Jesus more closely? Do you believe Jesus' promise that you will receive far more than you ever sacrifice to follow him?

Reflect and Respond

What is Jesus saying to me right now?

What step of faith is Jesus calling me to take today?

DAY 68

READ AND LISTEN: LUKE 18:31-43

Take a minute to listen for what the Spirit is saying in these verses…

COMMENT AND CONSIDER

After Peter's confession of Jesus as Messiah in the far north of Israel at Caesarea Philippi, Jesus began telling his disciples he was going to Jerusalem to die. (See Luke 9:22.) Even before that, when he was criticized for not fasting on the appointed days like John the Baptist and his disciples, Jesus alluded to his impending death when he replied, *"You can't make the wedding guests fast while the groom is with them, can you? But the time will come when the groom will be taken away from them—then they will fast in those days."* (Luke 5:34-35)

As they approached the ancient city of Jericho, just one day's journey from Jerusalem, Jesus took his closest disciples aside and told them exactly how and by whom he was going to be tortured and executed. He referred to biblical passages, such as the Suffering Servant in Isaiah 52-53, to assure them God was going to use all of this to bring about his Kingdom. He even predicted fulfillment of details in the prophecy such as, *"I gave my back to those who beat me, and my cheeks to those who tore out my beard. I did not hide my face from scorn and spitting."* (Isaiah 50:6)

This is the fourth time Luke records Jesus' explicit predictions of the grisly fate that awaited him in Jerusalem. (See also Luke 9:22, 44–45; 17:25.) At least three other times he alluded to his impending death. (See Luke 5:35; 12:49–50; 13:32–33.) As they drew closer and closer to Jerusalem, Jesus' sense of foreboding grew, and he couldn't get it out of his mind. He confided to his friends, *"I have a baptism to undergo, and how it consumes me until it is finished!"* (Luke 12:50) Despite all these predictions, allusions, and personal disclosures, Jesus' closest disciples still didn't get it! Luke tells us something was blocking their comprehension.

He describes the disciples' reaction to Jesus' first prediction of his death, *"But they did not understand this statement; it was concealed from them so that they could not grasp it, and they were afraid to ask him about it."* (Luke 9:45) Their whole lives they were told that when the Messiah came, he would destroy the enemies of Israel. Over and over again, they had seen the power of God flowing through Jesus to heal the sick, give sight to the blind, feed the multitudes, calm the storm, and even raise the dead! They had even experienced this power flowing through them. When some Samaritans refused them hospitality, James and John, the "Sons of Thunder," asked Jesus, *"Lord, do you want us to call down fire from heaven to consume them?"* (Luke 9:54) The disciples were certain this same divine power would flow through Jesus to overthrow Pontius Pilate and his oppressive regime once they reached Jerusalem. They were already jostling for their positions in his government. (See Mark 10:37.)

Jesus was trying to prepare his disciples for the disorienting earthquake that was about to engulf them, but they refused to go there and didn't want to even talk about it. We all have filters, and at times we consciously or subconsciously refuse to acknowledge things that are just too difficult to face. This seems to be what was going on with the disciples. It was like they were blind and refused to let Jesus open their eyes. It is perhaps ironic that the very next thing Jesus did was heal a blind man on the outskirts of Jericho! Despite barriers others put in his way, this man named Bartimaeus (see Mark 10:46) refused to be silenced and cried out all the more, *"Jesus, Son of David, have mercy on me!"* Jesus responded by opening his eyes. Perhaps Luke is telling us to emulate Bartimaeus rather than the twelve disciples.

What hard truths is Jesus revealing that you are filtering out and avoiding? How can you ask him to open your eyes so you will see and be prepared for the challenges that lie ahead?

REFLECT AND RESPOND

What is Jesus saying to me right now?

What step of faith is Jesus calling me to take today?

DAY 69

READ AND LISTEN: LUKE 19:1-10

Take a minute to listen for what the Spirit is saying in these verses…

COMMENT AND CONSIDER

As Jesus and his disciples approached Jericho from the north, he came to the New Testament-era city about a mile to the south of the abandoned hill of the ancient city. Already crowds had gathered along the main road which wound through the city on its way up to Jerusalem, pushing and jostling for position, hoping to catch a glimpse of the famous rabbi or even hear one of his amazing stories.

Undoubtedly the most reviled man in all of Jericho was a diminutive tax collector named Zacchaeus. Luke tells us he was the *"chief tax collector,"* which means he hired and supervised all the traitorous men who enforced the burdensome taxation of the Romans and Herodians and extorted honest, hard-working people for their own gain. On top of that, Zacchaeus was rich, which means he was very good at getting his minions to collect even more than the Romans demanded.

As Jesus and his disciples made their way south along the main pilgrim route toward Jericho, word had obviously reached the city that the famous teacher would soon be there. The leading Pharisee of the city was probably preparing to host a fancy banquet in Jesus' honor, in the hopes of gaining some of that honor for himself. But Zacchaeus made his own preparations for Jesus' arrival. Since he was a short man and the general population hated him, he knew no one would let him through to the front of the crowd. So, he decided to do something no self-respecting man would do in that culture. He ran ahead and climbed a tree! Just as running in public was considered inappropriate for a man of means and honor, so climbing a tree was considered child's play. Any adult male seen climbing a tree would open himself up for public ridicule.

Despite the social pressure, Zacchaeus ran ahead along the road and climbed a wide-branched fig-mulberry tree (*ficus sycōorus*) to see over the crowd in hopes of catching a glimpse of Jesus. Certainly, Zacchaeus had heard the scandalous rumors that Jesus called a former tax collector into his inner circle of disciples. Perhaps that radical forgiveness and unconditional grace planted a seed of hope in the chief tax collector's heart that he wasn't a completely lost cause after all. Maybe, just maybe, Jesus wouldn't condemn him like the people of Jericho had.

When Jesus saw this little man running and climbing, willing to become the butt of everyone's jokes just to catch a glimpse of him, he sensed something deeper was going on in Zacchaeus' heart. Just about the time the most prominent Pharisee would have approached Jesus with a flowery invitation to dine at his impressive home, Jesus abruptly stopped in front of that tree. Looking up, Jesus addressed this pariah by name, saying what no one in all of Jericho ever dreamed he would say, *"Zacchaeus, hurry and come down because today it is necessary for me to stay at your house."* The shock of the crowd would have been audible. How could Jesus even think of stepping across the threshold of an unclean tax collector's house, much less spend the night there?

Later that evening, Jesus reclined at Zacchaeus' table in a sign of true friendship, rather than at the table of the religious elites. Jesus' gracious acceptance of Zacchaeus, despite his obvious sin, moved this hardened and greedy man to a place of genuine repentance and faith. This change of heart led to radical acts of reparation—giving away half of his possessions and paying back four times what he had extorted, which was a lot! Jesus described this radical transformation by saying, *"Today salvation has come to this house because he too is a son of Abraham. For the Son of Man has come to seek and to save the lost."*

Are you willing to risk ridicule just to get a little closer to Jesus? What concrete steps could you take to demonstrate a repentant heart? Is there a table of friendship where you can demonstrate unconditional acceptance to the least likely in your community?

REFLECT AND RESPOND

What is Jesus saying to me right now?

What step of faith is Jesus calling me to take today?

DAY 70

READ AND LISTEN: LUKE 19:11-27

Take a minute to listen for what the Spirit is saying in these verses…

COMMENT AND CONSIDER

Jericho is the oldest continuously inhabited city in the world, stretching back about 10,000 years. By the time of Jesus, the Romans had conquered the Hasmonean city, and Mark Antony gifted it to his lover, Cleopatra of Egypt. When she fell out of favor with Rome, the Emperor Augustus passed it on to Herod the Great, who expanded the old Hasmonean residence into a lavish pleasure palace, complete with spa, swimming pool, and sunken gardens. The pilgrim road to Jerusalem ran through Jericho and then began climbing up into the Judean Desert, passing directly by Herod's lavish palace.

Like their father before them, Herod the Great's sons Archelaus, Antipas, and Philip traveled to Rome after he died in 4 BC to petition Augustus and the Senate, each seeking to take their father's place as "King of the Jews." When Jesus told a parable in which *"A nobleman traveled to a far country to receive for himself authority to be king and then to return,"* and they were about to pass by the Herodian palace, it wasn't hard to picture the scene!

When Jesus added the detail, *"But his subjects hated him and sent a delegation after him, saying, 'We don't want this man to rule over us,'"* the parallel was even clearer, because this is exactly what happened. Archelaus ordered his soldiers to violently put down demonstrations after his father's death and killed 3,000 Jews. A 50-person delegation traveled to Rome to beg Augustus not to give him royal power, but the Emperor compromised giving Archelaus half his father's kingdom and the title "ethnarch" rather than "king," forcing him to share power with his two brothers. Ten years later Archelaus had proved such a poor ruler he was deposed by the Romans who installed a governor in his place to rule Judea directly. The fifth of those Roman Governors was named Pontius Pilate.

In the parable the nobleman calls ten of his most trusted servants together and gives them each ten of his minas (about three years wages) with the instruction, *"Engage in business until I come back."* To engage in business means to buy goods in bulk, transport them where they are in demand, and sell them at a profit. It means to buy property, build on it, and sell it for more than it cost. It means to put the money to work in whatever creative way you can, so it multiplies and produces more money.

When the nobleman returned, he had been given authority to rule as king and called his servants to account. They each reported on what they had done with his capital and the return they had earned. Those who put the money to work were given positions of great authority in the new king's administration according to the return they earned. The one who earned ten minas was put in charge of ten cities, the one who earned five was now in charge of five cities! However, one of the servants was afraid of failing and being condemned, so he simply hid his ten minas and did nothing with them. As a result, this servant was not only excluded from ruling in the new kingdom, but what he had was taken and given to the most productive servant. If this is true with an evil and corrupt king, like the Herodians, how much more would a good and just God increase their authority based on their use of the capitals entrusted to them?

The disciples assumed Jesus was heading to Jerusalem to set up his new government and they were hoping for plum positions in his new administration. But Jesus made it clear he was going away and entrusting to them his capital to do business with until he returned. Then they would be given authority to rule in his Kingdom! Do you know what Jesus has given you to do Kingdom business with? What are you doing to multiply what he has entrusted to you? How are you letting fear keep you from taking wise risks with your capitals?

Reflect and Respond

What is Jesus saying to me right now?

What step of faith is Jesus calling me to take today?

DAY 71

READ AND LISTEN: LUKE 19:28-44

Take a minute to listen for what the Spirit is saying in these verses…

COMMENT AND CONSIDER

Jesus and the disciples departed Jericho, passed by Herod's palace, and began the day-long journey following the Roman road along the southern ridge of the deep desert valley called Wadi Qelt as it wound its way up through the mountains towards Jerusalem. Known as the "red ascent," both for the color of the sandstone hills and its bloody reputation as a bandit's hideout, this same treacherous road is the one taken by the unsuspecting traveler in Jesus' parable of the Good Samaritan.

Bethany was a Jewish village set on the eastern slope of the Mount of Olives, beyond which lay the great city of Jerusalem. Bethphage was another village a bit further up the slope of the mountain. Luke skips over the time Jesus and the disciples spent in Bethany with Mary, Martha, and Lazarus and the banquet in his honor hosted by Simon the Leper and moves straight to his very dramatic entrance into Jerusalem. (See John 12:1-11.)

It is clear Jesus made special preparations to enter Jerusalem in a profoundly symbolic way. The prophet Zechariah foretold how the Messiah would enter Jerusalem, *"Rejoice greatly, Daughter Zion! Shout in triumph, Daughter Jerusalem! Look, your King is coming to you; he is righteous and victorious, humble and riding on a donkey, on a colt, the foal of a donkey."* (Zechariah 9:9) For years now rumors had been flying around about Jesus' identity, with the big question being, "Is Jesus the Messiah?" To keep his mission from spiraling out of control and provoking immediate arrest, Jesus avoided directly identifying himself as the Messiah in public, though he had already affirmed his Messianic identity and calling to his inner circle of disciples. (See Luke 9:18-22.)

As he prepared to enter Jerusalem for his final Passover, Jesus knew this was the right moment to confirm the messianic rumors and make a public statement about his true identity. He had arranged ahead of time with some friends in Bethphage to have the colt of a donkey ready for him to ride into Jerusalem to fulfill Zechariah's prophecy. He sent two of his disciples into Bethphage with a secret password so the owners would know it was for him, *"If anyone asks you, 'Why are you untying it?' say this: 'The Lord needs it.'"*

When the crowds saw Jesus riding a young donkey over the Mount of Olives, they honored him as king by laying down their cloaks on the road, like we roll out a red carpet for dignitaries. They began singing a messianic song from Psalm 118:26, *"Blessed is the King who comes in the name of the Lord."* They knew he was claiming to be the Messiah, even if they didn't understand what kind of King he really was. They didn't realize Jesus was riding a young donkey and not a warhorse, because he came as the Prince of Peace, not a conquering military hero.

And yet, Jesus affirmed even this misinformed affirmation of his messianic mission from the people. When the Pharisees complained to him about this royal treatment Jesus simply replied, *"I tell you, if they were to keep silent, the stones would cry out."* When he crested the Mount of Olives and saw the Holy City with the glorious Temple laid out before him, he began to weep in prophetic sorrow for the destruction he knew was coming. If they had embraced his vision of the Kingdom of God rather than pursuing their own dreams of a kingdom of this world, they would have found a whole new abundant life. Instead, some 40 years later, the Jewish people finally tried to throw off Roman rule by force, leaving Jerusalem a smoldering ruin and the Temple a pile of rubble.

How do you recognize Jesus as your true King? Do you understand the nature of his rule? Are you ready to give your full allegiance to the Prince of Peace even if it means laying down your life?

Reflect and Respond

What is Jesus saying to me right now?

What step of faith is Jesus calling me to take today?

DAY 72

READ AND LISTEN: LUKE 19:45-20:8

Take a minute to listen for what the Spirit is saying in these verses…

COMMENT AND CONSIDER

In the tenth century BC, King Solomon built the first Temple in Jerusalem over the huge flat rock on the top of Mount Zion which his father had purchased for that purpose from Arunah the Jebusite. Ever since, it had been recognized by the Jews as the one place on earth where God's presence was fully manifested and the only place where efficacious sacrifices could be offered.

In 20 BC Herod the Great undertook a massive rebuilding and expansion of the Temple and its surrounding courts, turning it into one of the greatest religious structures of the ancient world. His engineers expanded the platform built at the top of Mount Zion to the size of 25 US football fields, completely engulfing the mountain. This plaza was surrounded by nearly a mile of porticoes held up by two rows of 30-foot-tall stone columns.

A series of barriers limited people's access to God's presence in the Holy of Holies, based on the religious category into which they fell. In the outer courts of this plaza, sacrificial animals were sold to worshipers. Jesus located his Jerusalem ministry in these Temple courts, coming there every day to teach the crowds and heal the broken. But that does not mean he affirmed how the Temple was run or the people who were running it.

When Jesus quoted Isaiah 56:7 and Jeremiah 7:11, he made a prophetic pronouncement that the Temple was meant to be a place where people of every background, Jews and Gentiles alike, could come and meet with God. However, the corrupt political leaders who colluded with the Romans and used their power to gain wealth, had turned the Temple courts into a segregated place of profiteering. By driving the merchants from the outer courts, Jesus was not attempting to change the economic practices of the Temple, for that would have provoked the Roman army to stop him. Instead, like the great biblical prophets who preceded him, he was enacting a symbolic condemnation of the religious establishment's system of categorizing people and limiting their access to God's presence.

This was a provocative act because the Temple was the power base of the most influential people in Jewish society at that time: the High Priest, the Chief Priests, and the Sadducees of the Sanhedrin. By controlling access to the sacrifices that ensured God's forgiveness and favor, these aristocratic priests exercised tremendous power over the Jewish people with the permission of Rome. So maintaining the smooth operation of the sacrificial system at the Temple was critical. That is why they demanded Jesus tell them by what authority he was doing this.

This was a risky act because both the priestly and rabbinical religious leaders were profoundly threatened by Jesus' popularity, authority, and power. For some time, they had been plotting how to get rid of Jesus, and this act cemented their determination to find a way to kill him during the Passover celebrations. But it was not going to be easy because Jesus had become so popular with the crowds who thronged into the Temple courts every day to listen to his profound teaching and witness his miraculous healings. They couldn't afford the political fallout of setting off a riot by arresting Jesus without pretense.

When they finally did engineer Jesus' execution, and he died on the cross, the Temple curtain separating the Holy of Holies from the Sanctuary inside the Temple was torn from top to bottom. This was the ultimate destruction of the barriers constructed by the religious leaders to control access to God and hold on to power for themselves. It was crystal clear by what authority Jesus was doing these things! As Jesus predicted, some forty years later the Roman destroyed the Temple stone by stone, never to be rebuilt even to this day.

Are you unconsciously participating in any religious systems or cultures that limit people's access to God's presence? Are you benefiting from the financial and social power these kinds of religious systems produce? What can you do to throw out the merchants from your own Temple courts and separate yourself from such corrupt religious cultures?

Reflect and Respond

What is Jesus saying to me right now?

What step of faith is Jesus calling me to take today?

Footsteps Every Week: Review

Write a brief summary of what Jesus said to you each day this past week and the step of faith he called you to take:

Monday

Tuesday

Wednesday

Thursday

Friday

Saturday

Footsteps Every Week: Reflect

Big Picture

As you look over what Jesus has said to you this past week, do you see any themes? What is the most important thing you need to remember and believe?

Predictable Pattern

As you look over what Jesus called you to do this past week, is there a new predictable pattern he is inviting you to establish in your life with God and others?

Plant the Word

As you look over the readings from this past week, write out the passage that feels most important for you and memorize it over the next week:

DAY 73

READ AND LISTEN: LUKE 20:9-19

Take a minute to listen for what the Spirit is saying in these verses…

COMMENT AND CONSIDER

Every day during that last Passover in Jerusalem, Jesus and his closest disciples walked 1.75 miles from Bethany where they were staying with Martha, Mary, and Lazarus, over the Mount of Olives, down through the Kidron Valley, and into the great Temple courts. It was typical for rabbis to gather people under the shade and shelter of the huge porticoes surrounding the Temple courts for times of teaching and dialogue. Certainly, this is where the huge crowds gathered to listen to Jesus' teaching and witness his miracles. This is also where religious leaders listened in and even confronted Jesus with thorny questions in order to find a pretense to arrest him. Over and over again, they tried to trick him into saying something by which he would indict himself, but they were foiled every time by Jesus' brilliant insights and irrefutable wisdom.

Most of Jesus' parables were designed to show us what it looks like to live as a part of God's Kingdom rather than the kingdoms of this world. However, during these final days, as the political opposition to his mission was growing, Jesus told a prophetic parable pointing to his coming fate and the guilt of those who would be responsible. In the Hebrew Scriptures, Israel is often portrayed as a vineyard owned and tended by the Lord. (See Isaiah 5:1-7.) Jesus picked up on that image as he confronted the corrupt religious leaders who were about to orchestrate his unjust execution.

In first-century Palestine, land ownership was concentrated in the hands of a relatively few wealthy families. As a result, many simple farming families didn't own the land they farmed but instead leased it from wealthy owners who lived elsewhere. Each harvest season the tenant farmers were expected to pay the owner a significant percentage of the fruit produced, which would be collected by the owner's servants. Often the owners mistreated and oppressed the farmers, but Jesus turned this upside down by framing the tenants as the ones mistreating the owner.

Each harvest, the owner sent his servants to collect their agreed percentage of the produce, but the ruthless tenants beat the servants and sent them away empty handed. After repeated abuse of his servants, the owner decides to send his *"beloved son,"* expecting them to respect his position in the family. However, the tenants do exactly the opposite. Hoping they can usurp his ownership of the vineyard, they take the son outside the walls of the vineyard and kill him. With his grace and patience finally exhausted, the owner of the vineyard brings these terrible tenants to justice, executing them and ensuring ownership of the vineyard passes to those who will be good stewards of it.

The symbolism of the story is obvious to those of us who know that Jesus, the beloved son of the Father, was rejected, like so many prophets before him, and taken outside the walls of Jerusalem and brutally executed. Even without the hindsight of history, those who first heard the story knew it was an indictment of the religious leaders who rejected Jesus' vision of the Kingdom. When some of the hearers reacted to the harsh ending of Jesus' story, he quoted Psalm 118: 22-23, *"The stone that the builders rejected has become the cornerstone."*

This passage takes on even more prophetic meaning when we realize the rock of Golgotha on which Jesus was crucified is a spire of fissured limestone left by ancient builders who quarried around the unsuitable building material, leaving behind a twenty-foot-tall rocky outcropping which the Romans chose as their place of execution. Jesus the builder was literally crucified outside the walls of Jerusalem on the stone which the builders rejected! Jesus said we can either submit to him as the foundation and cornerstone of the new reality he is building by laying down our lives *("be broken to pieces")*, or we will end up facing judgment like those vicious tenant farmers *("it will shatter him")*.

Are you seeking to become a more fruitful and faithful tenant in the Father's vineyard? In what ways have you slipped into trying to take ownership of the vineyard for yourself? Are you going to fall on the Rock of Jesus and be broken to pieces, or will he have to shatter you?

Reflect and Respond

What is Jesus saying to me right now?

What step of faith is Jesus calling me to take today?

DAY 74

READ AND LISTEN: LUKE 20:20-40

Take a minute to listen for what the Spirit is saying in these verses...

COMMENT AND CONSIDER

As the day of Passover approached, the crowds listening to Jesus teach and watching him heal in the Temple courts continued to grow in size and intensity. The religious leaders' determination to get rid of Jesus also grew. They moved from simply spying on Jesus' teaching to directly confronting him with questions designed to incriminate him.

Ever since the Roman general, Pompey, first conquered Palestine in 63 BC, the Jewish people had been seething under excessive Roman taxation in various forms. The poll tax, a fixed annual payment required of every non-Roman citizen in the provinces, was the most hated of all Roman taxes. In AD 6, when Jesus was about ten years old, Judas the Galilean led a violent revolt against the Romans in protest of that poll tax. The rebellion was brutally put down by the Roman legions, and hundreds of Jewish men were crucified along the Via Maris, which ran through Sepphoris, near Nazareth.

When the leaders asked Jesus, *"Is it lawful for us to pay taxes to Caesar or not?"* it was a loaded political question. If Jesus undermined the Imperial collection of taxes, they could brand him as a traitor and a rebel. If Jesus affirmed Roman taxation, he could be discredited to nationalist groups such as the Zealots, who claimed paying taxes to Rome was akin to treason.

Despite using exaggerated flattery, their destructive purpose was obvious to Jesus, so he diverted attention from the politics by asking for a common Roman denarius, equivalent to one day's wages. The face of the coin featured a portrait of Emperor Tiberius and an inscription that read, "Tiberius Caesar, Augustus, son of the divine Augustus." Pointing out that this coin bore the image of Caesar, Jesus answered their question by saying, *"give to Caesar the things that are Caesar's, and to God the things that are God's."*

Jesus' brilliant reply reached all the way back to Genesis 1, telling them to obey the laws of Rome in so far as they don't violate the Law of God, but not to offer full allegiance to Rome. Paying Roman taxes was nothing more than giving back to Caesar that which bore his image. But recognizing you bear the image of God means you owe everything to the God who created you!

Next the Sadducees decided to take their shot at Jesus with a theological question. The priestly Sadducees only followed the first five books of the Law of Moses, while the Pharisees accepted all the written Hebrew Scriptures, as well as the Oral Law passed down by the rabbis. Because the resurrection of the dead is only explicitly taught in the later books of the Old Testament, the Sadducees did not believe in the afterlife. So they tried to discredit Jesus, who believed in the resurrection, by describing a scenario in which resurrection from the dead would be rendered ridiculous.

Levirate marriage is the law requiring a man to marry his deceased brother's wife to provide offspring for him. (See Deuteronomy 25:5–10.) In a society where lots of children were critical to the success of an extended family's business, and sons ensured the continuation of your genealogical line, this made sense. However, the Sadducees described a scenario in which seven brothers died one after the other, and each one married the same widow in turn. They pointed out that if the resurrection is real, there is no way to determine whose wife she would be in the afterlife.

Jesus reframed the entire scenario by pointing out that marriage does not apply to the life to come because we will be *"like the angels."* Furthermore, Jesus quoted the very Scriptures the Sadducees followed in which the LORD is described as *"the God of Abraham and the God of Isaac and the God of Jacob..."* As he explained, *"He is not the God of the dead but of the living, because all are living to him."*

Do you know how to engage with those who want to discredit your beliefs? Are you prepared to answer for your faith when challenged? What can you learn about this from following Jesus' example?

Reflect and Respond

What is Jesus saying to me right now?

What step of faith is Jesus calling me to take today?

DAY 75

READ AND LISTEN: LUKE 20:41-21:4

Take a minute to listen for what the Spirit is saying in these verses...

COMMENT AND CONSIDER

One night God sent the prophet Nathan to deliver a message to King David: *"The Lord declares to you: 'When your time comes and you rest with your ancestors, I will raise up after you your descendant, who will come from your body, and I will establish his kingdom.'"* (2 Samuel 7: 11-12) This was the basis for the many biblical prophecies that God would raise up a descendant of David to establish his eternal Kingdom and rule over all of creation. This "Son of David" became known as "the anointed One," which is "Messiah" in Hebrew and "Christ" in Greek.

After being on the defensive by responding to trick questions from his opponents in the Temple courts, Jesus went on the offensive by challenging their commonly held assumptions about the nature of this promised Messiah. He quoted Psalm 110:1, *"The Lord declared to my Lord, 'Sit at my right hand until I make your enemies your footstool.'"* David is the author of this messianic Psalm, which means he is addressing the Messiah as *"my Lord."* Jesus raised the question of why King David would refer to his own son as *"my Lord."* Jesus was showing us the Messiah is more than simply a human king but is greater than the greatest human king ever to rule Israel.

Jesus regularly referred to himself as "the Son of Man," a clear reference to Daniel's vision of *"one like a son of man was coming with the clouds of heaven... His dominion is an everlasting dominion that will not pass away, and his kingdom is one that will not be destroyed.* (Daniel 7:13-14) Normally "son of man" simply meant an ordinary human being, but in Daniel's vision it describes someone who looks like an ordinary human being but is, in fact, a heavenly being.

Jesus' question about Psalm 110 pointed to himself as the divine King of the universe who will establish God's eternal reign. It is not surprising that this Psalm is the Scripture passage most often quoted by the writers of the New Testament who testified to Jesus' full humanity and his full divinity!

John recorded a similar teaching in these very same Temple courts when Jesus told his detractors, *"Truly I tell you, before Abraham was, I am."* (John 8:58)

After challenging the crowd's theological assumptions, Jesus began to address the spiritual celebrity so often nurtured by the teachers of the law. He told his disciples to beware of those who use their religious position to gain social status and power. Recognized rabbis were entitled to wear special long robes with tassels on the corners of the hem, much like the clerical uniforms worn by the clergy of certain traditions today. They expected to be addressed in public with the honorary greeting required of a person with inferior social status to their superior. They expected to be seated in the special seats near the front of the synagogue and in the seats of honor closest to the host at banquets. All these social cues reinforced the idea that they were more important than "ordinary" people.

Jesus called out these self-aggrandizing teachers for the hypocrisy of making a show of their long, pious prayers in public, while at the same time taking financial advantage of widows, the most vulnerable members of society. In contrast he pointed out a poor widow who offered two simple pennies for the Temple treasury but gave a far greater gift than that of the rich donors seeking public recognition because *"all these people have put in gifts out of their surplus, but she out of her poverty has put in all she had to live on."*

Although Jesus was God in human flesh, he didn't lift himself above others or make others feel less important. His deep humility is an indictment of religious pride and an example for all who seek to follow him.

Do you recognize Jesus as both human and divine? How does Jesus' example teach you to see yourself relative to others? How can you reject special status and learn to live in genuine humility?

Reflect and Respond

What is Jesus saying to me right now?

What step of faith is Jesus calling me to take today?

DAY 76

READ AND LISTEN: LUKE 21:5-38
Take a minute to listen for what the Spirit is saying in these verses…

COMMENT AND CONSIDER
As Jesus and his disciples entered and exited the huge and beautifully constructed Temple complex, they craned their necks to look at the soaring stonework some 180 feet above their heads, oohing and aahing just as we do today when we visit Jerusalem. Jesus responded to their admiring remarks with a shocking statement, *"These things that you see—the days will come when not one stone will be left on another that will not be thrown down."* Herod the Great had started his massive expansion of the Temple complex some 50 years earlier, and archaeological evidence shows they were still working on it at the time of Jesus. The size of the buildings and the quality of the workmanship were unprecedented, with some stones exceeding 500 tons! The assumption was this structure would endure for many centuries.

Jesus' provocative statement evoked questions from the disciples about how and when this destruction would happen. Jesus' response included predictions of things that would happen in their lifetimes, along with things that have still not happened 2,000 years later. This is typical of biblical prophecy which often warned of events that were just about to take place, but also conveyed a deeper meaning which still applies to things that have not yet happened. It is not always easy to separate the immediate predictions from the future fulfillment without the benefit of hindsight.

Looking back, we can see Jesus was predicting the Roman siege of Jerusalem in AD 70 when four legions surrounded the city, eventually breaking through the walls, burning the city, and tearing down every single structure Herod built on the Temple Mount. We can also see Jesus foretold intense persecution that would come in wave after wave for the first three centuries of the movement he began. But at the same time, he described supernatural cosmic events that have yet to take place, when he will return in glory to conquer sin, death, hell, and the devil once and for all, fully establishing his eternal and perfect rule over all of creation.

It is important to learn how to recognize the layers of meaning in these prophetic words of Jesus so we are not deceived. Jesus explicitly warned us false messiahs and natural phenomena such as earthquakes, famines, and plagues are not signs that his return is imminent. He also pointed out that conflict between nations is not the defining event, *"When you hear of wars and rebellions, don't be alarmed. Indeed, it is necessary that these things take place first, but the end won't come right away."* The point here is that we don't know the day or hour when all this will take place but must wait and watch in faith.

Jesus' purpose in these apocalyptic teachings was not to give us the timeline or the details, but to prepare us for what is to come and to teach us how to live with both the expectation of his return and the assurance that he will complete the mission he has begun. Human history has a trajectory, and it is heading inevitably toward the fulfillment of God's good and perfect will for all of creation. This is the fulfillment of the Kingdom which Jesus inaugurated and which he will return to complete. But we live in between the inauguration and fulfillment of God's good and gracious rule. Following Jesus in the power of his Spirit as an extended spiritual family is how we learn to live in that Kingdom today and how we prepare ourselves for the fulfillment of that Kingdom that is sure to come. As Jesus said, *"be alert at all times, praying that you may have strength to escape all these things that are going to take place and to stand before the Son of Man."*

Do you live with an expectation of how history is going to end? How does that awareness or lack of awareness affect the way you are living today? What can you do today to live in the Kingdom of God more fully, so you are prepared for Jesus' return?

Reflect and Respond

What is Jesus saying to me right now?

What step of faith is Jesus calling me to take today?

DAY 77

READ AND LISTEN: LUKE 22:1-13
Take a minute to listen for what the Spirit is saying in these verses…

COMMENT AND CONSIDER

Every spring first-century Jews celebrated their redemption from slavery in Egypt with a special Passover meal at sundown on the 14th of Nisan in the Hebrew calendar, followed by a seven-day holiday known as "The Festival of Unleavened Bread." During the week leading up to this most important of all Jewish holidays, pilgrims poured into Jerusalem and filled up the Temple courts, mesmerized by Jesus' teaching and healing. The religious leaders had determined the only way to maintain their own power was to put Jesus to death. Due to Jesus' popularity with the throngs of pilgrims, they were afraid to arrest him openly, so they decided to find a quiet moment when the crowds had all gone away to arrest Jesus and convince Pontius Pilate, the Roman Governor, to execute him.

We don't know what human reasons moved Judas, one of Jesus' most trusted disciples, to help the authorities arrest Jesus privately. Perhaps one of the members of the Sanhedrin had approached him with hints of financial reward. Some have suggested Judas was disillusioned with Jesus' lack of political and military initiative and decided he was a false Messiah. Due to Judas' extreme remorse after Jesus' arrest (see Matthew 27:3-5), it seems more likely he hoped to force Jesus' hand by betraying him, assuming Jesus would resort to force once faced with self-preservation. In any case, Luke explains the deeper spiritual reality by simply writing, *"Then Satan entered Judas…"*

The chief priests were powerful members of the aristocratic priestly families of Jerusalem who controlled the sacrificial functions of the Temple complex. They had at their disposal a militia of Levitical priests, "the temple police," who were authorized to maintain security on the Temple Mount and to enforce the judgments of the Sanhedrin, the Jewish council of 70. Judas agreed to betray Jesus by informing these religious leaders where he would be when the crowds had gone away.

Jesus was fully aware the religious authorities were plotting to kill him, and he became prophetically aware one of his own disciples was going to betray him to them. Jesus made special arrangements for his disciples to share the Passover meal at a large home inside the walls of Jerusalem and wanted to be sure nothing would interfere with his plans for that night. For that reason, Jesus kept the location of their meal secret, even from the disciples, so he would not be betrayed and arrested before completing everything the Father had sent him to do.

He chose Peter and John to prepare the Passover meal at this secret location. Rather than risk telling them where it was and tipping off his betrayer, Jesus told them to enter the city, look for a man carrying a jar of water, follow him and knock on the door he entered saying, *"The Teacher asks you, 'Where is the guest room where I can eat the Passover with my disciples?'"* Just like the donkey in Bethpage, Jesus set up a secret password to assure the owner these were, in fact, his disciples.

Coming over the Mount of Olives from Bethany, Peter and John entered the walled city through the Spring Gate on a street filled with people carrying jars of water. How were the disciples to recognize this particular messenger? In a patriarchal society, carrying water was considered women's work, so all the people carrying water jars would have been women, except for the one who would lead them to their location. When their host heard the password and showed them a large upper room in the spacious house, they prepared for the special meal.

Have you ever compromised your values to make something happen you thought was God's will? How did that work out? What are some ways Satan may have a foothold in your life, pushing you to take control rather than let go and trust Jesus? Are there strategic ways you can intentionally prepare for these challenges to make sure they don't keep you from following Jesus?

Reflect and Respond

What is Jesus saying to me right now?

What step of faith is Jesus calling me to take today?

DAY 78

READ AND LISTEN: LUKE 22:14-23
Take a minute to listen for what the Spirit is saying in these verses…

COMMENT AND CONSIDER
Strong biblical, historical, and archaeological evidence points to the foundations of a large first-century Jewish home in a priestly neighborhood on the southwest hill of Jerusalem as the location of Jesus' final Passover meal with his disciples. This was the home of Mary, the mother of John Mark, a relative of Barnabas and part of a priestly family from Cyprus. When Jesus gathered there with his closest friends, he expressed just how important this meal was, *"I have fervently desired to eat this Passover with you before I suffer. For I tell you, I will not eat it again until it is fulfilled in the kingdom of God."*

John tells us Jesus began this most important evening by scandalously washing the disciples' feet and challenging them to do the same. (See John 13:1-15.) Then they reclined on pillows around a low, three-sided table called a triclinium, set with loaves of unleavened bread, cups for wine, bowls of bitter herbs, and a sweet fruit mixture. Traditionally, the Passover meal retold the story of the Exodus in which God miraculously redeemed the people of Israel from slavery in Egypt. In that day, they marked the doorposts of their homes with the blood of a lamb so the angel of death would pass over them and strike down the first-born males of Egypt instead.

Earlier in the day, Peter and John went to the Temple Mount, bought a lamb, took it through the inner courts to the priests who slaughtered it, sprinkling the blood on the altar and returning the carcass to the disciples. They then returned to the house on the southwest hill where they roasted the lamb in preparation for the meal. The meal was typically hosted by the male head of the family, in this case Jesus, retelling the Exodus story as they ate the food and drank from four symbolic cups of wine. After the second cup of wine, they ate the roast lamb, and Jesus began to give a new interpretation of the meal.

He took the unleavened bread and, instead of referring to the hurried nature of the Exodus when there was no time for the bread to rise, he prayed the traditional prayer of thanks, broke the bread, and gave it to them saying, *"This is my body, which is given for you. Do this in remembrance of me."* Then he took the third cup of wine, traditionally known as "the Cup of Redemption," gave thanks, and gave it to them to drink saying, *"This cup is the new covenant in my blood, which is poured out for you."*

It is hard to imagine what Jesus' disciples were thinking and feeling in that moment. They were all vividly aware they had just eaten the sacrificial lamb whose body was broken and blood was shed for their redemption. Perhaps they remembered what John the Baptist declared years earlier when he first saw Jesus at the Jordan River: *"Look, the Lamb of God, who takes away the sin of the world!"* (John 1:29) But then, as their heads were swimming trying to comprehend what all this could mean, Jesus gave the heart-breaking prophecy that one of them, his closest friends, was going to betray him. This immediately sent them all into a tailspin, arguing among themselves who it could be.

In first-century culture, sharing a meal together was a covenantal act, binding the participants together in a special relationship. It is clear Jesus established the New Covenant, ratified by his own blood, through this meal. Centuries earlier God promised, *"I will make a new covenant with the house of Israel and with the house of Judah… I will put my teaching within them and write it on their hearts. I will be their God, and they will be my people."* (Jeremiah 31:31-33)

What does it mean for you to participate in this special covenantal meal 2,000 years later? How can your experience of Communion help you love and follow Jesus more closely?

Reflect and Respond
What is Jesus saying to me right now?

What step of faith is Jesus calling me to take today?

Footsteps Every Week: Review

Write a brief summary of what Jesus said to you each day this past week and the step of faith he called you to take:

Monday

Tuesday

Wednesday

Thursday

Friday

Saturday

Footsteps Every Week: Reflect

Big Picture

As you look over what Jesus has said to you this past week, do you see any themes? What is the most important thing you need to remember and believe?

Predictable Pattern

As you look over what Jesus called you to do this past week, is there a new predictable pattern he is inviting you to establish in your life with God and others?

Plant the Word

As you look over the readings from this past week, write out the passage that feels most important for you and memorize it over the next week:

DAY 79

READ AND LISTEN: LUKE 22:24-38
Take a minute to listen for what the Spirit is saying in these verses...

COMMENT AND CONSIDER
While Jesus foretold his impending death through broken bread and poured out wine, the disciples argued over who was the greatest. Talk about missing the point! Rather than pull out his beard hair, Jesus patiently explained to them one more time the nature of the Kingdom he had consistently demonstrated to them. He used the hierarchy of pagan kings to explain the way things work in the kingdoms of this world versus the Kingdom of God.

The Roman Empire was the dominant superpower of the Mediterranean world and had imposed its authoritarian system on people as far away as North Africa and the Middle East. Rome was ruled by powerful aristocratic families who owned vast tracts of land worked by peasant farmers who were dependent on their wealthy benefactors for provision. These lords of Rome held onto power by keeping their serfs subservient, doling out just enough provision to keep them from utter poverty.

Jesus operated in exactly the opposite way with his disciples. Rather than holding on to power by keeping his disciples dependent on him for provision, he freely gave power away. The whole point of Jesus' call to follow was to raise them up and empower them to do everything he did. He even went so far as to say, *"Truly I tell you, the one who believes in me will also do the works that I do. And he will do even greater works than these, because I am going to the Father."* (John 14:12) When Jesus sent his disciples out on mission, they came back amazed to report they were able to heal the sick just as they had seen Jesus do so many times! (See Luke 10:17-20.)

Jesus showed them greatness in God's Kingdom is not measured by how much status and power you can acquire for yourself, but how much you multiply God's Kingdom by investing in disciple-making disciples and empowering them to do everything you do that looks like Jesus. This happens when we are willing to let go of control, lay down our lives, and give God the glory for everything. Rather than becoming power-hungry benefactors who keep people dependent on us, we are to become empowering servants who raise others up and release them to do even more than we can by ourselves. That is what Jesus did, and it changed the world!

This does not mean we will be left with nothing. Jesus reminded the disciples of his promise that the whole Kingdom was theirs. (See Luke 12:32.) By laying down their lives and giving power away, they would ensure for themselves a place of responsibility and authority in God's Kingdom of servants. Those who are willing to follow Jesus by taking up their cross and laying down their lives will sit at the King's table and represent the God of the universe for eternity! Jesus warned the disciples Satan would tempt them to choose the way of the benefactor rather than his Way. He predicted that Simon would fail the test, but told him if he was willing to repent, he could turn back and strengthen his brothers.

Jesus also warned them real conflict was coming, and they would need to defend themselves. Earlier Jesus had told them when struck on one cheek to turn the other cheek (see Luke 6:29), but now he told them to buy a sword! This is a little confusing because later that night Simon drew a sword to protect him, but Jesus told them to put away their swords. (See Luke 22:49-51.) Apparently, there is a time to fight and a time to lay down our arms, and we will have to discern in the moment what self-giving love demands. (See Ecclesiastes 3:1-8.)

How have you slipped into the role of benefactor, holding on to power by keeping others dependent on you? What will it mean for you to let go of control, give away power, and invest in others so they learn to do even greater things than you?

REFLECT AND RESPOND

What is Jesus saying to me right now?

What step of faith is Jesus calling me to take today?

DAY 80

READ AND LISTEN: LUKE 22:39-53

Take a minute to listen for what the Spirit is saying in these verses…

COMMENT AND CONSIDER

After finishing the Passover meal, Jesus led his disciples from the upper room in the home of Mary, mother of John Mark, on the southwest hill of Jerusalem, eastward down through the Kidron Valley, heading toward the Mount of Olives. When it was too late to walk all the way back to Bethany, they sometimes slept on the mountain overlooking the Temple Mount, perhaps in a large cave near the Garden of Gethsemane that housed an olive press. As they went, Jesus continued to teach them profound truths, explaining how abiding in him leads to a life of fruitfulness and describing the role of the Holy Spirit, the Counselor, who was coming to fill them. After praying for his followers and those who would follow them, they arrived at Gethsemane. (See John 15-17.)

The Garden of Gethsemane was an olive orchard situated at the foot of the Mount of Olives in an area where olive oil was produced. There is still a grove of ancient olive trees growing there, at least a thousand years old, under the careful watch of Franciscan monks. This seems to be the area where Jesus and the disciples normally came when they spent the night on the mountain, because Luke uses the phrase *"as usual,"* and Judas knew exactly where to find them after he discovered they had left the upper room. (See John 18:2.) The main group of disciples settled down for the night, and Jesus invited his three closest disciples, Simon, Andrew, and John, to join him in the grove. Asking them to pray for him and warning them to resist temptation, he went further and began to pour out his heart to the Father.

Jesus knelt and prayed a powerfully honest prayer of relinquishment, *"Father, if you are willing, take this cup away from me—nevertheless, not my will, but yours, be done."* Drinking the cup is a biblical metaphor for enduring suffering and punishment. (See Isaiah 51:22 and Mark 10:38.) Matthew and Mark record Jesus praying this prayer three times, followed each time by the discovery of his closest three disciples sleeping rather than supporting him in prayer. (See Matthew 26:36-46 and Mark 14:32-42.)

Luke focuses instead on the intensity of Jesus' struggle in prayer, describing an angel who appeared to strengthen Jesus in this battle between his flesh and spirit. As a physician, Luke also described the physical manifestation of blood mingling with his sweat, a medical condition resulting from extreme stress known in both ancient and modern times as *hematidrosis*. Gethsemane means "place of olive pressing," and huge stones used to press oil from olives in the first century have been discovered there. As Jesus faced the final step toward his suffering and death, it was as if he were being crushed under the weight of that impending fate.

It would have been easy for Jesus to simply slip away into the night and disappear over the Mount of Olives into the vast Judean desert which he knew so well from his forty days in the wilderness. Instead, by honestly pouring out his anguish to the Father and choosing to relinquish his will, Jesus found the strength he needed to face this final leg of his long journey to the cross.

At that very moment, Judas appeared, leading a mob of priests, temple police, and members of the Sanhedrin who had come to arrest him in the darkness. Judas approached Jesus and betrayed him with a kiss on the cheek, which in Middle Eastern culture is the standard greeting of love and respect between friends. Peter tried to defend Jesus with his sword, cutting off the ear of Malchus, the high priest's servant. (See John 18:10.) Jesus rebuked Peter and healed the man's ear, determined to submit to his dark fate rather than fight.

How aware are you of the ongoing tug-of-war in your heart and soul between what you want in your flesh and your commitment to do God's will? How can prayer help you win that battle? What can you learn from Jesus' example in Gethsemane?

Reflect and Respond

What is Jesus saying to me right now?

What step of faith is Jesus calling me to take today?

DAY 81

READ AND LISTEN: LUKE 22:54-62

Take a minute to listen for what the Spirit is saying in these verses…

COMMENT AND CONSIDER

The religious leaders bribed Judas to reveal Jesus' location late on the night the holiday was beginning, when the crowds were dispersed and asleep in their own homes after the celebration of the Passover. Failing to find him in the upper room of the house of Mary, the mother of John Mark, Judas led the chief priests and their police officers to the base of the Mount of Olives where Jesus and the disciples often spent the night. There they arrested Jesus and dragged him back across the Kidron Valley, into the walled city of Jerusalem.

Although all the disciples fled when Jesus was arrested, Peter and John had the courage to follow the temple police at a distance to see where they were taking him. According to the rabbinical rules recorded in the Mishnah at a later period, the Sanhedrin could only carry out trials in the Chamber of Hewn Stone, a room in the inner courts of the Temple. But this was no ordinary trial, so the religious authorities brought Jesus back up to the southwest hill, to the large, extended family home of Annas the former High Priest (See John 18:13), and his son-in-law Caiaphas, the current High Priest.

Extended family homes in the time of Jesus were built as multiple rooms around a central courtyard accessed by a strong outer gate. The courtyard is where the family gathered, where meals were cooked and eaten, and where fires were built in the colder months. Wealthy families used this same floor plan but built larger homes with more two-story rooms around the courtyard. The soldiers took Jesus into the High Priest's home and up to a large upper room overlooking the courtyard. Peter and John managed to gain access to the courtyard and went into the very heart of the home where Jesus was going to be tried by members of the Sanhedrin. They sat around the fire with the household slaves and soldiers, warming themselves. (See John 18:15-18.)

Jesus prophesied all the disciples would desert him and scatter when he was arrested, but Peter insisted he would not, even under pain of death. Jesus told Peter directly, *"I tell you, Peter, the rooster will not crow today until you deny three times that you know me."* (Luke 22:34) Perhaps the reason Peter brandished his sword to defend Jesus and took the risk of entering the home of Caiaphas while Jesus was on trial was his determination not to deny Jesus as predicted. But as the conversation unfolded around the fire, Peter found himself being sifted just as Jesus had foretold. (See Luke 22:31-32.)

In the flickering light of the fire, one of the servant girls saw Peter's illuminated face and recognized him as a follower of Jesus. But Peter denied it, *"Woman, I don't know him."* A little later someone else identified him as a disciple of Jesus, but he said, *"Man, I am not!"* About an hour later, someone connected Peter to Jesus by his distinctive Galilean accent, but Peter cried out, *"Man, I don't know what you're talking about!"* At that moment a rooster crowed, and Jesus looked down into the courtyard from the upper room, catching Peter's eye. Overwhelmed by the realization he had denied Jesus three times exactly as predicted, Peter left the courtyard weeping bitterly.

Judas' betrayal and Peter's denials were similar failures of character, but their responses to these failures were completely different. Judas was so overcome with guilt and shame for betraying Jesus to the authorities he killed himself. (See Matthew 27:3-5.) Peter, on the other hand, recalled Jesus' promise to him at the last supper, *"I have prayed for you that your faith may not fail. And you, when you have turned back, strengthen your brothers."* (Luke 22:32) That is exactly what he did—he repented, was restored, and became the leader of the disciples. (See John 21:1-19.)

Have you made bold promises like Peter did, only to crumble under the pressure when tested? How do you handle your failures? Do you carry guilt and shame like Judas or receive grace and restoration like Peter?

Reflect and Respond

What is Jesus saying to me right now?

What step of faith is Jesus calling me to take today?

DAY 82

READ AND LISTEN: LUKE 22:63-71

Take a minute to listen for what the Spirit is saying in these verses…

COMMENT AND CONSIDER

The Sanhedrin was the council of 70 elders in Jerusalem who ruled over Jewish affairs at the time of Jesus. The High Priest, appointed by the Roman Governor, presided over this council made up of both Sadducees and Pharisees. They were the most powerful group of Jewish leaders in Palestine but did not have the power to impose capital punishment. The High Priests who led the Sanhedrin had to placate Rome since these leaders could be deposed at any time for not towing the party line—and often they were!

The High Priest who presided over the Sanhedrin when Jesus was arrested was Joseph ben Caiaphas ("Caiaphas" in the New Testament), a member of the most powerful priestly family of his time. The three High Priests who preceded him lasted no more than one year in office, but Caiaphas ruled for 18 years, from AD 18-36, a testimony to his political savvy. His father-in-law, Ananus ben Seth, ("Annas" in the New Testament) was the first High Priest appointed by the Romans and ruled from AD 6-15. Even after he was no longer officially High Priest, Annas continued to exert significant influence through his six sons who held the office of High Priest, in addition to his son-in-law Caiaphas! This is why Jesus was taken to see Annas before being brought before Caiaphas and the Sanhedrin. (See John 18:13.)

Caiaphas and the Sanhedrin had monitored Jesus' activities for years, but after he raised Lazarus from the dead, they intentionally looked for a way to put Jesus to death, even though he was wildly popular and they did not have the authority to carry out executions. Their many attempts to bait Jesus into arguments or trap him with trick questions had failed miserably. Finally, with the help of Judas, they accomplished their goal of arresting Jesus when no crowds were around to witness it, and now they had to condemn him before word spread of his arrest.

In the Mishnah, which is an account of the rabbis' teachings written down about AD 200, a chapter called "Tractate Sanhedrin" describes how the Council of 70 operated. It clearly reflects idealized memories of the first century but may also contain accurate historical information. That Tractate contains a number of rules governing a capital trial, including the stipulation that cases were to be tried during daylight hours, held in the Chamber of Hewn Stone, not held on the eve of a festival, begin with evidence for acquittal, not to finalize a conviction on the same day as the trial, and require the agreement of at least two witnesses. It is possible not all of these rules were in force at the time of Jesus, but they fit the context of the first century and very well may have been. Not one of these rules was followed in the Sanhedrin's examination and condemnation of Jesus.

Luke gives us a simplified account of this patently illegal trial, but he describes the vicious physical abuse and mockery of Jesus' obvious prophetic gifts. Jesus refused to validate this illegitimate proceeding by defending himself but would not deny his true identity as Messiah and Son of God. Instead, he prophesied, *"But from now on, the Son of Man will be seated at the right hand of the power of God."* Although they could find no legal basis for his condemnation, they accused him of blasphemy, using this as their excuse for condemning him to death. Since this sham trial in the middle of the night was obviously illegal, they reconvened after sunrise to attempt to legitimize their decision and prepare to ask Pilate to do their dirty work for them.

Have you ever manipulated a system to get the outcome you wanted? Have you ever been the victim of people who misused their power to falsely accuse and condemn you? What does Jesus' response or lack thereof teach you about yourself?

Reflect and Respond

What is Jesus saying to me right now?

What step of faith is Jesus calling me to take today?

DAY 83

READ AND LISTEN: LUKE 23:1-12
Take a minute to listen for what the Spirit is saying in these verses...

COMMENT AND CONSIDER
In AD 26, during the reign of Emperor Tiberius Caesar, Pontius Pilate was nominated to become the fifth governor of Judea by his friend Lucius Aelius Sejanus. Sejanus rose in power to become the leader of the Praetorian Guard in Rome and Tiberius' closest advisor. After Tiberius withdrew to the island of Capri and turned over the administration of the Empire to others, Sejanus was named Consul with Tiberius, making him a de facto co-ruler. This put Pilate in a strong position because his benefactor in Rome was the most powerful man in the Empire. Sejanus was known for his antisemitic policies, which meant Pilate didn't have to worry about negative repercussions if he mistreated his Jewish subjects.

We see this attitude played out in Pilate's aggressive stance toward his subjects. Ignoring Jewish sensibilities, he brought pagan military standards into the city of Jerusalem under the cover of night, sparking a massive riot. Other examples include taking funds from the Temple treasury to build an aqueduct, killing a group of rebellious Galileans in the Temple courts (see Luke 13:1), and wiping out a group of Samaritans who gathered when a prophet claimed to have uncovered sacred vessels buried by Moses.

However, Pilate's heavy-handed administration of Judea was mitigated by a dramatic shift in power back in Rome. On October 18, AD 31, his patron Sejanus conspired to take sole control of the Empire and was swiftly executed along with his supporters after Tiberius discovered the plot. Suddenly, Pilate was now without a powerful friend back in Rome, which put him in a vulnerable position, and he had to take a more moderate stance toward his Jewish subjects. In the end, he was recalled to Rome in AD 36 because of his overreaction to the Samaritan prophet.

In the early morning hours, Roman officials typically made themselves available to rule on disputes between their subjects. Pilate normally governed Judea from the coastal city of Caesarea, but during the festivals he took up residence in the enormous Herodian palace on the western hill of Jerusalem to oversee the crowds that gathered for the holidays. Archaeologists have discovered the remains of a huge plaza on the grounds of that palace that featured a raised judgment platform at each end. This is where, early that Friday morning, the religious leaders brought Jesus before Pilate in an effort to convince him to execute Jesus. (See John 19:13.)

The members of the Sanhedrin had condemned Jesus for blasphemy because he did not deny he was the Messiah, the Son of God. However, Pilate considered this an internal Jewish religious matter not meriting the death penalty, particularly in his politically weakened position. This is why Caiaphas had to bring a different charge to convince Pilate to execute Jesus. Pilate's main job as Governor was to maintain order (Latin: *Pax Romana*) so that taxes and goods continued to flow back to Rome. The charge that Jesus made himself out to be a king and opposed the paying of taxes was a direct challenge to Rome's rule designed to evoke a response from Pilate.

Despite these inflammatory charges, Pilate found no credible evidence to convict Jesus based on his cross-examination, saying *"I find no grounds for charging this man."* In a classic case of passing the buck, Pilate suddenly remembered Jesus was from Galilee and Herod Antipas, the ruler of Galilee, was in Jerusalem for the Passover festival. He sent Jesus to Herod hoping to wipe his hands of the matter. However, because Jesus refused to engage with Antipas and perform tricks for him, Herod simply mocked Jesus and sent him back to Pilate. The Roman leaders' mutual fear of Jesus' popularity and the threat he posed to their rule cemented a new friendship between these old enemies.

What will you do to keep control of the things you value the most? Are you liable to be manipulated by others because you feel vulnerable? In what ways have you slipped into acting like Pilate?

Reflect and Respond

What is Jesus saying to me right now?

What step of faith is Jesus calling me to take today?

DAY 84

READ AND LISTEN: LUKE 23:13-31
Take a minute to listen for what the Spirit is saying in these verses…

COMMENT AND CONSIDER
A carefully curated crowd of people, gathered by the religious leaders, stood in the huge plaza of the Palace of Herod the Great before the raised judgment platform where Pontius Pilate considered the accusations brought against Jesus. Pilate had sent the prisoner to Herod Antipas, since Jesus came from his territory of Galilee, hoping to rid himself of this politically charged hot potato. However, Herod sent Jesus back, and now Pilate knew he had to resolve the situation. Since he found no evidence of wrongdoing and Antipas had not condemned Jesus for any crime, Pilate decided he would simply have Jesus beaten and then released.

The Romans performed three different kinds of beatings as legal punishment. The first was the *fustes*, which was a lighter beating, functioning as a symbolic warning. The second was the *flagella*, which was more severe and inflicted injury. The third was the *verbera*, which was the most severe whipping carried out with a wooden handle that had multiple strips of leather embedded with bits of metal or bone attached to it, which could tear the flesh right off the victim's back. This kind of scourging could result in death through blood loss or exposure of internal organs.

Luke's language indicates Pilate intended to levy the lightest of these three punishments, the *fustes*, and then use his power of clemency and the tradition of releasing a popular prisoner during the Passover holiday to placate the crowds. But this crowd would have none of that. They wanted one thing—Jesus hanging from a cross. Instead, the crowd called for the release of Barabbas, an insurrectionist who had committed multiple murders as part of a campaign of terror in the city that sought to destabilize the Roman occupation and foment armed revolt. Pilate tried to reason with the crowd, but they shouted him down with cries of *"Crucify! Crucify him!"*

Once more Pilate tried to convince the crowd that a light beating and holiday release was the appropriate compromise, but in the end, he caved to popular opinion and political pressure. Pilate had given in to political pressure from the Jewish population before, and here we see him do so again. He chose political self-preservation over what he knew was right and knowingly condemned an innocent man to the worst kind of torturous death, a Roman crucifixion.

Victims of Roman crucifixion were made to carry the crossbeam of their cross on their shoulders through the streets to the place of execution to heighten the deterrence factor of this terrifying mode of death. As Jesus wound his way through the streets of Jerusalem carrying the crossbeam toward the Gennath ("Garden") Gate in the northwest wall of the city, a crowd gathered to witness the grisly parade. At one point a passerby from Cyrene in North Africa (modern Libya) was conscripted by the Roman soldiers to carry the crossbeam, implying Jesus collapsed under the weight of the beam, probably due to blood loss and sleep deprivation.

As this nightmarish scene unfolded, Jesus continued to focus on those around him rather than himself. Women in the crowd cried out and lamented the abuse being heaped on Jesus. He was a man like none other, who had affirmed their worth as bearers of God's image and welcomed them as his followers when society did not recognize women disciples. Jesus cried out to them, *"Daughters of Jerusalem, do not weep for me, but weep for yourselves and your children."* Then Jesus began to prophesy over them the suffering that would come with the Roman destruction of the city. If Jesus' crucifixion was bringing them grief now, in some forty years they would see thousands of men crucified in these very streets.

When have you given in to peer pressure and failed to do the right thing in order to be accepted by others? Have you ever been caught up in a crowd mentality and done things you later regretted? When you face injustice and suffering, how much do you focus on yourself rather than others?

Reflect and Respond

What is Jesus saying to me right now?

What step of faith is Jesus calling me to take today?

Footsteps Every Week: Review

Write a brief summary of what Jesus said to you each day this past week and the step of faith he called you to take:

Monday

Tuesday

Wednesday

Thursday

Friday

Saturday

Footsteps Every Week: Reflect

Big Picture
As you look over what Jesus has said to you this past week, do you see any themes? What is the most important thing you need to remember and believe?

Predictable Pattern
As you look over what Jesus called you to do this past week, is there a new predictable pattern he is inviting you to establish in your life with God and others?

Plant the Word
As you look over the readings from this past week, write out the passage that feels most important for you and memorize it over the next week:

DAY 85

READ AND LISTEN: LUKE 23:32-43
Take a minute to listen for what the Spirit is saying in these verses…

COMMENT AND CONSIDER
In an ancient rock quarry outside the northwestern wall of first-century Jerusalem, ancient builders cut the large limestone blocks used to rebuild the Temple after the return of the exiles from Babylon in the sixth century BC. The quarrying marks can still be seen underneath the current Church of the Holy Sepulcher built on that site in the fourth century AD. This quarry slipped into disuse over the centuries, and by the time of Jesus it was converted into a cemetery for wealthy families with tombs cut into the rock walls.

When the original builders quarried the stone, they came across a section of limestone that was fissured and unstable, not suitable for building. As a result, they cut around that section, leaving a 20-foot-tall rocky outcropping in the middle of the quarry. When the Romans looked for a place of crucifixion, they chose this large rock, referred to as *Golgotha*, Aramaic for "place of the skull." It was just outside the city wall and located along a road leading from the Gennath Gate to the city of Joppa on the coast. This meant crucifixions carried out at Golgotha were witnessed by many residents of Jerusalem, satisfying one of the main purposes of crucifixion: terrifying the local population into submission to Rome.

When the victim of crucifixion arrived at the place of execution, they were stripped of all their clothes, their arms were stretched out on the crossbeam, and they were tied or nailed through the wrists with large iron spikes, carefully avoiding the major arteries to prevent a quick and easy death. Then the crossbeam was lifted and hung on the vertical post, which was already wedged into a hole in the rock. The victim's feet were tied or nailed through the heel bone to the upright post. The weight of the body pulling down on the arms constricted the lungs from pumping out excess fluid as they normally do. This resulted in a slow build-up of fluid in the lungs, making it harder and harder to fill the lungs with air.

The victim of crucifixion would pull themselves up with their arms and push up with their legs, taking the pressure off their lungs so they could get a breath of air. Then they would slump back down with the weight of their body pulling the muscles tight around their lungs once again. Since scourging was a required precursor to crucifixion, the victim's torn back would scrape up and down along the rough post as they pulled against the nail wounds in their wrists and ankles, causing intense pain. As Jesus was crucified, he was slowly drowning in his own fluids while torturing himself just to take a breath. It is hard to imagine a more inhumane form of execution.

In the midst of this unimaginable pain, Jesus showed supernatural grace toward his torturers when he prayed for the Roman soldiers, *"Father, forgive them, because they do not know what they are doing."* Jesus was not alone in his suffering. Two others who had been rightly convicted of banditry were being crucified on either side of Jesus. One criminal berated and mocked Jesus, while the other rebuked his partner in crime, confessed his sins, and begged, *"Jesus, remember me when you come into your kingdom."* Jesus' powerful reply was a promise for all who recognize our need for grace and forgiveness: *"Truly I tell you, today you will be with me in paradise."*

Jesus chose to lay down his life as a sacrifice for others. As he said, *"No one has greater love than this: to lay down his life for his friends."* (John 15:13) In Jesus' willing suffering on the cross, forgiving his tormentors, and promising eternity to a dying criminal, we see the unconditional love of God displayed more clearly and more powerfully than anywhere else. Are you unaware of the forgiveness you so desperately need? Are you asking Jesus to remember you in his eternal Kingdom? Wherever you find yourself, know that you are loved more than you can possibly begin to imagine!

Reflect and Respond

What is Jesus saying to me right now?

What step of faith is Jesus calling me to take today?

DAY 86

READ AND LISTEN: LUKE 23:44-56
Take a minute to listen for what the Spirit is saying in these verses…

COMMENT AND CONSIDER

The Gospels tell us Jesus was nailed to the cross around 9:00 AM and that he died around 3:00 PM, suffering for a total of about 6 hours. (See Mark 15:25.) There was an eclipse of the sun, and earthquakes shook the ground. The huge curtain that separated the Holy of Holies from the rest of the Temple was torn from top to bottom. Josephus tells us the curtain was thirty feet square, as thick as the width of a man's hand, woven in beautiful blue, purple, and scarlet colors with golden threads forming an intricate design of heavenly creatures. The tearing of this curtain was a powerful sign that God's presence would no longer be limited to a building of stone, but now the Spirit of God would dwell in the hearts and lives of his people!

While he hung on the cross, Jesus meditated on Psalm 22, which he quoted when crying out, *"My God, my God, why have you abandoned me?"* (Mark 15:34) This Psalm of lament gave voice to Jesus' suffering, but also offered hope because it ends with powerful promises of God's faithfulness. Luke tells us Jesus also meditated on Psalm 31:5, which he quoted when he said, *"Father, into your hands I entrust my spirit."* This prayer of faith reflects the assuring message of the entire Psalm which finishes, *"Be strong, and let your heart be courageous, all you who put your hope in the Lord."* (Psalm 31:24)

Despite all he was suffering, Jesus put his hope in the Lord and entrusted himself to his heavenly Father to the end. The way Jesus faithfully endured his suffering, expressed honest grief, showed grace to his captors, offered hope to the repentant thief, cared about those around him, and breathed his last breath impacted the hardened Roman centurion so deeply he exclaimed, *"This man really was righteous!"*

Another witness of these things was a wealthy and powerful man named Joseph of Arimathea, a member of the Sanhedrin. He had come to believe in Jesus but kept his faith in the shadows for political expediency. In the moment of Jesus' death, Joseph stepped out of the shadows and into the harsh light of association with a man who had just been executed for treason. Casting aside his fears of what the repercussions might be, Joseph went directly to Pilate and asked for the body of Jesus. He offered his new family tomb as a place where Jesus' body could be honorably interred rather than thrown on the burning garbage heap in the Hinnom Valley.

In the first century, Jews who could afford it anointed the bodies of their dead and placed them on either a shelf or in a slot cut into the walls of a rock tomb. The most expensive tombs had a large disc-shaped stone that rolled down a track carved in the rock to seal the door of the tomb. Joseph, with the help of a Pharisee named Nicodemus (see John 19:39), anointed Jesus' body with oil and spices, wrapped it in linen cloth, laid it on the rock-cut shelf in his tomb, and rolled the stone to seal it shut. The women disciples of Jesus carefully watched all this from a distance.

Earlier Jesus quoted the Suffering Servant prophecies from Isaiah to explain the meaning of his impending death. (See Luke 22:37.) At first, followers must have been completely shocked and bewildered by Jesus' crucifixion, but after his resurrection Jesus explained his death was an atoning sacrifice that once and for all paid the price for our sins. As Isaiah prophesied, *"But he was pierced because of our rebellion, crushed because of our iniquities; punishment for our peace was on him, and we are healed by his wounds."* (Isaiah 53:5)

What does the death of Jesus on the cross mean for you? How does the tearing of the curtain in the Temple affect your relationship with God? Are you standing in the shadows or willing to be counted with Jesus no matter what the consequences?

Reflect and Respond

What is Jesus saying to me right now?

What step of faith is Jesus calling me to take today?

DAY 87

READ AND LISTEN: LUKE 24:1-12

Take a minute to listen for what the Spirit is saying in these verses…

COMMENT AND CONSIDER

Jesus was radically counter-cultural for recognizing women as equal in value to men. In a culture where women had no rights apart from their father or husband, Jesus interacted with women of all different social classes as unique individuals in their own rights. In a society where the religious elites treated women as second-class citizens to be avoided as unclean, Jesus embraced women as members of his spiritual family and called them to be his disciples.

Because of this, it is not surprising Jesus' closest female disciples were fiercely devoted to him. The Samaritan woman at the well went into her village and told everyone about the man who knew everything she had ever done! (See John 4:1-30.) After Jesus cast seven demons out of Mary Magdalene, she followed him all the way to Golgotha and the empty tomb. (See Luke 8:1-3.) After Jesus affirmed Mary of Bethany for taking the posture of a disciple, she poured out costly oil on Jesus' feet as a sign of her devotion. (See Luke 10: 38-42 and John 12:1-7.)

While the male disciples scattered when he was arrested and only John was at the cross, the women disciples were there in force, led by Mary Magdalene. (See Luke 23:55.) Jesus' mother Mary had chosen not to stand with him in Nazareth and thought he had gone crazy, but now Mary stood at the foot of the cross watching her son die. (See Luke 4:16-30; Mark 3:20-21, 31-35; John 19:25.) The women disciples were so determined to be true to their Lord, they went out early on Sunday morning to honor Jesus one last time by anointing his body.

As they headed to the tomb in the predawn darkness, they must have wondered how the Roman soldiers guarding the tomb would react to their demand to roll back the stone and reopen the tomb. But to their surprise and shock, when they arrived the stone was already rolled back, and there was no body in the tomb! Luke tells us they were *"perplexed"* about this, wondering what had happened. John tells us they assumed someone had stolen Jesus' body. (See John 20:13.)

Suddenly two angels, shining in white, appeared to the women disciples saying, *"Why are you looking for the living among the dead? He is not here, but he has risen!"* Then the angels reminded the women of Jesus' predictions that he would die, but then rise from the dead. Although they had repressed this memory, now it came rushing back to them. Jesus was not dead but fully alive just as he had promised! This changed everything. Jesus' death was not a shattered dream and failed mission, but a critical part of God's plan to overcome sin, death, hell, and the devil. Jesus' resurrection confirmed the truth of everything he ever said and did. This power for new life would spark a movement of everyday people who were empowered to change the world!

We can just imagine the overwhelming joy that propelled the women back to the upper room to report what they had experienced. But suddenly they were snapped back to the patriarchal reality of the first century in which a woman's testimony was considered suspect. As Luke says it, *But these words seemed like nonsense to them, and they did not believe the women.* To Peter's and John's (see John 20:3) credit, they acted on the women's testimony, ran to the tomb, and found exactly what they had described. It would still take a direct encounter with the risen Jesus before any of them were fully convinced it was not too good to be true, but they were well on their way to a whole new kind of life.

What does it say about Jesus that women were the first to hear the Good News of his resurrection and encounter their risen Lord? What do you do when others don't accept your testimony of the power of Jesus in your life?

Reflect and Respond

What is Jesus saying to me right now?

What step of faith is Jesus calling me to take today?

DAY 88

READ AND LISTEN: LUKE 24:13-27

Take a minute to listen for what the Spirit is saying in these verses…

COMMENT AND CONSIDER

During the Passover people who lived in surrounding villages often traveled into the Holy City to worship in the Temple, listen to the rabbis teaching in the Temple courts, and celebrate the Passover meal with a family who lived inside the walls of Jerusalem, if possible. Cleopas and his companion (an unnamed friend or perhaps his wife?) lived in a village called Emmaus, which was about seven miles from Jerusalem. There are two possible sites for Emmaus, but so far, we don't have conclusive evidence confirming the exact location of this village.

Cleopas and his friend/wife were followers of Jesus who had spent the Passover in Jerusalem, listening to Jesus' teaching and celebrating the holiday with their spiritual brothers and sisters. However, things quickly spiraled out of control when they woke up on Friday morning to the news that Jesus had been arrested in the night and was now being tried by the Roman Governor at Herod's Palace. When news of Jesus' crucifixion reached them, there must have been chaos among the followers of Jesus, with people seeking refuge wherever they could, hoping the authorities were not coming for them next. Cleopas and his friend ended up staying in the large home of Mary, the mother of John Mark, along with Jesus' closest disciples.

Once the Sabbath had passed, they were awakened on Sunday morning by the report of Mary Magdalene and the other women disciples who had visited the tomb and discovered it empty, except for two angels who told them Jesus was not dead, but alive! Cleopas must have been among those men who doubted the women's report. (See Luke 24:11.) Later that day, as they walked those seven miles home, Cleopas and his companion discussed these disorienting events, arguing about what it all meant. If the unnamed disciple was Cleopas' wife, perhaps she wanted to believe the women's report of angels announcing Jesus' resurrection, while Cleopas remained skeptical.

In any case, they were deeply discouraged—when suddenly, the risen Jesus joined them along the way and began to engage in their discussion, although they did not recognize him! Even Jesus' closest disciples often did not immediately know it was him when they met the risen Jesus. He was transformed from his normal earthly body into his eternal resurrection body and apparently looked different, although he still bore the unmistakable marks of his crucifixion. (See 1 Corinthians 15:35-49 and John 20:20, 27.) Jesus may have been purposely preventing them from recognizing him at the time. As Cleopas summarized the tumultuous events of the past three days, he expressed his deep disappointment in Jesus' death by saying, *"But we were hoping that he was the one who was about to redeem Israel."*

Jesus quickly rebuked him saying, *"How foolish you are, and how slow to believe all that the prophets have spoken! Wasn't it necessary for the Messiah to suffer these things and enter into his glory?"* Then he proceeded to show them all the places in the Old Testament that point to a Messiah who would suffer and die in order to redeem humanity and establish God's reign.

Certainly, the Servant Songs of Isaiah were a major part of this amazing Bible study! (See Isaiah 50:4–9; 52:13–53:12.) While teaching on the Temple mount, Jesus quoted Psalm 118 after telling a parable about his death, highlighting *The stone that the builders rejected has become the cornerstone.* (Psalm 118:22) While on the cross, Jesus quoted from Psalm 22, which reads like a description of his crucifixion. The early followers of Jesus also pointed to Psalms 2 and 16 as prophecies about a suffering Messiah. Perhaps they learned these insights from the risen Jesus.

Are you naturally more skeptical or more believing when you hear others testify to the power of God in their lives? Are you open to discovering new insights into Jesus that contradict your assumptions about him? Will you let Jesus help you to interpret the Bible more accurately?

REFLECT AND RESPOND

What is Jesus saying to me right now?

What step of faith is Jesus calling me to take today?

DAY 89

READ AND LISTEN: LUKE 24:28-35

Take a minute to listen for what the Spirit is saying in these verses…

COMMENT AND CONSIDER

As Cleopas and his unnamed companion came to the outskirts of Emmaus, their mysterious traveling companion seemed as if he were going further. He had just led them through the most mind-blowing Bible study they had ever experienced, and they didn't want it to end! In Middle Eastern culture, hospitality is one of the highest values. And in the ancient world, travel at night was rare and dangerous. Since it was nearly evening, it was natural for them to invite him to come and stay with them for the night.

In that culture, covenants were how people related to each other. A covenant is the bond created between people who make promises to each other and trust those promises. Meals were often the symbolic way these covenants were ratified and renewed. Every year, on the 15th of Nisan in the lunar calendar, the Jewish people celebrate the Passover meal, which is an annual renewal of the Covenant God first made with his people through the blood of the lamb. Each week Jews gather after sundown on the Sabbath to share a meal together, remembering and renewing the Covenant God made with them at Sinai. These special meals were a foreshadowing of the Messianic Banquet foretold by the prophets in which the Messiah will gather all God's family together for the feast of feasts that never ends! (See Isaiah 25:6-9 and 55:1-5.)

Because of this, inviting someone into your home to share a meal was a significant act that was not treated lightly. It was an offer of covenantal friendship. When they invited this traveler into their home and to their table, they were saying, "we want to be more connected to you." When they took their places around the table, surprisingly the mysterious visitor assumed the role of host, normally reserved for the male head of the family. He took the bread in his hands, broke it, and said the traditional prayer of thanks, "Blessed are you Lord our God, King of the universe, for you have given us the fruit of the earth to eat." As he went through these familiar rituals and spoke these familiar words, something began to stir in Cleopas and his companion.

Whatever had prevented them from recognizing Jesus as he spoke to them on the road was suddenly lifted, and they realized who he was. They could hardly believe their eyes! The women were right. What the angels told them was true. The same Jesus who had been nailed to a cross, bled, died, and buried, was now fully alive before them! And just as suddenly as they recognized him, he disappeared from their midst. It was not an apparition or vision. It was not a ghost or non-material spirit. Jesus was really, physically present to them. They spoke with him and they sat with him. He broke the bread and prayed the prayer. But he was clearly changed, transformed, glorified!

As they struggled to take in all that was happening, they realized something was different about this man from the moment they first met him on the road. They reflected to each other, *"Weren't our hearts burning within us while he was talking with us on the road and explaining the Scriptures to us?"* They got straight up from the table and made the seven-mile journey back into Jerusalem as quickly as they could. They went to the upper room at the home of Mary, the mother of John Mark, and were amazed to discover the risen Jesus had appeared to Simon as well! (See 1 Corinthians 15:5.) Then Cleopas and those who were with him confirmed Simon's testimony by reporting how Jesus had met them on the road, explained the Scriptures to them, and was revealed in the breaking of bread.

Do you sometimes fail to recognize Jesus in your midst? What would it mean for you to invite him into your home, your family, your life more fully? How can the breaking of bread with Jesus and others open your eyes to his presence in a new way?

Reflect and Respond

What is Jesus saying to me right now?

What step of faith is Jesus calling me to take today?

DAY 90

READ AND LISTEN: LUKE 24:36-53
Take a minute to listen for what the Spirit is saying in these verses…

COMMENT AND CONSIDER

It is hard to imagine just how disorienting and overwhelming the events of that Passover week in Jerusalem were for Jesus' disciples. It began with Jesus' exhilarating entrance to Jerusalem on the Mount of Olives and continued through the week in his teaching, healing, and sparring with the religious leaders in the massive Temple courts. The intensity built when Jesus reinterpreted the Passover meal, sweat blood in the Garden of Gethsemane, and was betrayed by Judas and condemned by the religious leaders. But the sentencing by Pilate, the death of Jesus on the cross, and the sealing of his body in Joseph's tomb dealt the final blow to the men and women who had followed Jesus for the past three years.

Crushed, disillusioned, terrified, and trapped in the deepest, darkest valley of despair, the followers of Jesus were initially bewildered by the women's report that the tomb was empty and angels claimed Jesus was alive. But now they were catapulted into the stratosphere of hope and joy by multiple encounters with the risen Jesus! First the women who met Jesus near the empty tomb, followed by Simon. Then the disciples from Emmaus and now, even as Cleopas was telling their amazing story, Jesus himself stood among them!

How would you react if the person you saw die three days earlier was now unmistakably alive and standing before you? No wonder Jesus' first words to them were, *"Peace to you!"* Luke tells us they were *"startled and terrified"* and assumed this must be some kind of disembodied spirit. Jesus immediately reassured them it was him and he was real, saying *"Look at my hands and my feet, that it is I myself! Touch me and see, because a ghost does not have flesh and bones as you can see I have."* Then he held out his arms so they could see the marks of the nails where he had been crucified.

This was irrefutable physical evidence that the same Jesus who was nailed to the cross and died was now fully alive and standing before them gloriously transformed. However, their heads were still spinning with questions and doubts, so Jesus ate a piece of leftover fish from their dinner to give further evidence he was real. Then he reminded them how many times he had foretold his death and resurrection and pointed out it was foretold by the Old Testament prophets. Then he opened their minds so they could begin to comprehend the Scriptural message that *"The Messiah will suffer and rise from the dead the third day, and repentance for forgiveness of sins will be proclaimed in his name to all the nations, beginning at Jerusalem."*

The resurrection of Jesus is not some tall tale rooted in the wishful thinking of people who had a vision of a non-material spirit. The same Jesus who was crucified, died, and was buried in Jerusalem, appeared to many different people many different times in many different places, and offered irrefutable evidence it was really him, he was physically present, and he is truly alive! His body is different than ours, the first example of what the new creation will be like, far greater than any reality we know. This was not a conspiracy cooked up by the disciples to build their status and fame. Nearly all of Jesus' closest followers eventually paid with their very lives for the testimony they had seen him alive. Who will die for something they know is a lie?

Jesus is truly risen from the dead, and that means everything he ever said is true, he has the power to fulfill every promise he ever made, and he is the one person in all human history worth following, trusting, and worshiping with all our heart. He showed us the way we are meant to live, poured out his Spirit to empower us in living that Jesus-shaped life, and will return one day to bring God's Kingdom to fulfillment!

How does the reality of Jesus' resurrection affect you today? Are you willing to trust and follow him no matter what, as those first disciples did?

REFLECT AND RESPOND

What is Jesus saying to me right now?

What step of faith is Jesus calling me to take today?

Footsteps Every Week: Review

Write a brief summary of what Jesus said to you each day this past week and the step of faith he called you to take:

Monday

Tuesday

Wednesday

Thursday

Friday

Saturday

Footsteps Every Week: Reflect

Big Picture
As you look over what Jesus has said to you this past week, do you see any themes? What is the most important thing you need to remember and believe?

Predictable Pattern
As you look over what Jesus called you to do this past week, is there a new predictable pattern he is inviting you to establish in your life with God and others?

Plant the Word
As you look over the readings from this past week, write out the passage that feels most important for you and memorize it over the next week:

MORE RESOURCES BY BOB ROGNLIEN TO HELP YOU FOLLOW JESUS

Find them all at www.bobrognlien.com

❖ **Books** | *Footsteps Every Day: Matthew, Mark, John*
  ➢ Continue the journey you have begun with daily Gospel readings and reflections on the Way of Jesus, illuminated by insights from history, archaeology, and culture. These three books of daily devotions together with the current volume can take you through all four Gospels in one year.

❖ **Book** | *Recovering the Way: How Ancient Discoveries Help Us Follow the Footsteps of Jesus*
  ➢ An in-depth treatment of Jesus' life illuminated by the history of his time, the cultural background of his world, and archaeological discoveries from our time. Includes over 100 photos, reconstruction drawings, and maps. Excellent for serious students and teachers who want to go deeper.

❖ **Book** | *The Most Extraordinary Life: Discovering the Real Jesus*
  ➢ A shorter telling of the true story of Jesus from his baptism to his resurrection, informed by history, archaeology, and culture. Each chapter begins with an expanded account of an event from Jesus' life which reads like a historical novel. Written for everyday people who know Jesus and those who want to get to know him for the first time.

❖ **Video** | *Recovering the Way: The Video Series*
  ➢ An in-depth video teaching series that illuminates the life of Jesus with thousands of full color photos, reconstruction drawings, and animated maps. The twelve 45-minute

episodes correspond to the twelve chapters in the book, *Recovering the Way* (see above) and will bring the Way of Jesus to life for you.

❖ **Trip** | *The Footsteps of Jesus Experience*
> ➢ A 14-day journey through Israel and Palestine, following the life of Jesus from birth to resurrection. We keep the group relatively small, stay in unique Christian guesthouses, drive ourselves in vans, do lots of walking off the beaten path, focus on the historically verifiable sites, and keep an intentionally spiritual focus. It is not a tour, but an intensive pilgrimage.

❖ **Podcast** | *The Footsteps Podcast with Bob Rognlien and Matt Switzer*
> ➢ In each episode Footsteps Experience leaders Bob and Matt take you on a journey to a significant site in the Holy Land and show how the discoveries there bring a specific biblical passage to life with new insights and applications.

❖ **Trip** | *The Footsteps of Paul Experience*
> ➢ A 15-day journey from Antioch to Corinth through Turkey and Greece, following the missional journeys of the Apostle Paul and his disciples. We keep the group relatively small, stay in boutique hotels with historical and cultural charm, drive ourselves in vans, go off the beaten path, focus on the historically verifiable sites, and keep an intentionally spiritual focus. It is not a tour, but an intensive pilgrimage.

❖ **Book** | *A Jesus-Shaped Life: Discipleship and Mission for Everyday People*
> ➢ A practical guide to putting the Way of Jesus into practice in your everyday life with the people who are closest to you. It tells the story of how Bob and Pam learned to pattern their lives and their family more intentionally after Jesus. It

also offers practical tools, vehicles, and strategies to make discipleship and mission a part of your daily life.

❖ **Book** | *Empowering Missional Disciples*
> ➢ A resource for leaders who want to help those they lead to live a life that looks more like Jesus and produces more of the fruit he produced. Includes lots of field-tested tools and vehicles for multiplying missional disciples.